I Require Proof: A Sovereign Guide to Breaking Presumption and Exposing False Authority

Sovereign Action, Volume 2

Roger Davies

Published by TWON Publications, 2025.

I REQUIRE PROOF: A SOVEREIGN GUIDE TO BREAKING PRESUMPTION AND EXPOSING FALSE AUTHORITY

First edition. November 29, 2025.

ISBN: 979-8232030704

Written by Roger Davies.

Table of Contents

Dedication

To every man and woman who refuses assumption, who asks for truth, and who stands in their own authority. Your calm awareness protects you. Your clarity exposes false power. Your refusal to be moved keeps the path open for others who wish to live free.

Epigraph

Authority ends when truth is questioned.Proof is the voice of the living.

Introduction

Proof is the foundation of truth. Without proof, all that remains is assumption. Modern systems depend on assumption because assumption is easy. It does not need evidence. It does not need authority. It does not need open agreement. It grows through silence, routine, and fear. Many people accept demands because they think they must. They comply because they believe the one making the claim stands above them. They accept terms that were never spoken. They follow instructions that were never proven. This is the world created by assumption.

A living man or living woman walks a different path. The living does not obey assumption. The living does not accept pressure without question. The living does not submit to claims that cannot be proven. The living stands in clarity. When someone makes a claim, the living asks for evidence. When someone states authority, the living asks for its source. When someone presents terms, the living asks whether they were agreed. Proof is the line between truth and illusion. Proof is the difference between personal authority and adopted authority.

Systems rarely offer proof. They offer the appearance of proof. They use letters with strong language. They use automated notices. They use procedures that look official. They use titles that give the image of certainty. These tools work only when the living accepts them without question. The moment the living asks for evidence, the image cracks. The structure weakens. The authority that seemed solid begins to look uncertain. This happens because many claims do not stand on truth. They stand on habit. They stand on pressure. They stand on the hope that the living will not question them.

Asking for proof is not conflict. It is clarity. Clarity protects the living from assumption. Clarity stops false authority from attaching itself. Clarity prevents silent contracts. The living does not need to shout. The living does not need anger. The living does not need defiance. A single question asked calmly is stronger than any reaction. Proof is a simple request. It is a natural request. If a claim is valid, it can be proven. If a claim is weak, the request exposes it.

In the artificial world, assumption travels faster than truth. People accept claims because they do not pause. They react before they think. They fear consequences that do not exist. They believe in authority that has not been shown. They accept obligations that were never agreed. These habits are taught from childhood. Schools teach obedience. Workplaces teach compliance. Society teaches acceptance. Over time this conditioning becomes automatic. The living forgets how to question. The living forgets how to stand. The living forgets the simple strength of asking for clarity.

Proof brings the mind back to awareness. It forces the interaction into the open. It requires the claimant to show their foundation. Many cannot. They rely on confidence rather than truth. They rely on tone rather than evidence. They rely on pressure rather than substance. When proof is required, these tools lose impact. Pressure does not replace evidence. Tone does not replace truth. Confidence does not replace authority. Proof is the only standard that matters.

The living understands the difference between appearance and reality. The artificial world creates appearance. Paperwork creates appearance. Uniforms create appearance. Titles create appearance. These appearances influence behaviour. They make claims look stronger. They make demands look lawful. They make expectation look mandatory. Proof cuts through all of this. Proof asks one simple question. Is the claim true. If it is, the claimant can show it. If it is not, the claim dissolves.

Asking for proof also protects inner peace. Fear grows when the mind believes it must obey. Fear grows when a letter is seen as a threat. Fear grows when language is taken as truth. When the living requires proof, the fear breaks. The mind moves from reaction to reflection. Reflection reveals that many threats are empty. It reveals that authority must be shown. It reveals that pressure is a tactic, not a truth. This shift changes everything. Fear loses its control. The living begins to see clearly.

Requiring proof is not an act of resistance. It is an act of self-respect. It is the living saying, show me the truth before you expect anything from me. It is the living standing in dignity. It is the living protecting their own boundaries. It is the living acknowledging that they do not belong to any system. Systems can request participation. They cannot demand it without evidence. Asking for proof places responsibility on the claimant. Responsibility is avoided only by those who lack authority.

Requiring proof is also a reminder to the world that the living is not confused. Confusion helps systems claim power. Confusion makes people easier to guide. Confusion creates silent agreement. When the living removes confusion through simple questions, assumption collapses. The artificial world thrives on speed, pressure, and reaction. The sovereign mind uses stillness, clarity, and questions. One approach fuels false authority. The other ends it.

This path is not about finding ways to defeat systems. It is about understanding how they function. It is about seeing the difference between what is real and what is assumed. It is about recognising that many claims rely on the living staying silent. Silence looks like agreement. Agreement looks like consent. Consent looks like obligation. When the living speaks, the chain breaks.

Asking for proof is the simplest way to dismantle false authority. It is the foundation of conscious living. It is the beginning of real sovereignty. Sovereignty is not found in conflict. It is found in clarity. It is found in stillness. It is found in awareness. It is found in the space between reaction and truth. Proof brings the living back to that space.

The living does not accept assumption. The living does not accept unwanted terms. The living does not accept pressure without question. The living does not accept authority without origin. The living requires proof.

And where there is no proof, there is no authority.

The Nature of Proof

Proof is the foundation of truth. Without proof, nothing claimed has weight. Words are air. Demands are noise. Threats are pressure. Proof separates truth from assumption. Proof turns questions into clarity. Proof gives the living a place to stand. Without proof, the world becomes a landscape of influence rather than understanding. People act out of fear rather than awareness. They comply because they think they must, not because truth demands it.

The living requires proof because the living stands in truth. Truth is not shaken by tone. Truth is not shaped by pressure. Truth is not altered by confidence. Truth needs no force behind it. Truth needs no threat. Truth is simple. It reveals itself. When truth is behind a claim, the evidence is clear. When assumption is behind a claim, the evidence is absent. This is why asking for proof is powerful. It exposes what is real and what is invented.

Systems use assumption because assumption saves effort. Systems do not want to prove their authority every time they make a claim. They rely on the living acting automatically. They rely on compliance through routine. They rely on people mistaking confidence for authority. They rely on silence from the living. Silence can be used to create the impression that the claim has been accepted. This is why assumption survives. It grows in the spaces where questions are not asked.

Proof breaks this cycle. When the living asks for proof, the dynamic shifts. The claimant now carries the burden of evidence. The claimant must show the foundation of their claim. Many claims do not survive this test. They collapse when examined. They look strong only when left unchallenged. They look lawful only when no one asks for the source of authority. They look certain only when the living reacts rather than reflects.

The living who understands the nature of proof becomes difficult to manipulate. They no longer react to printed words. They no longer respond to tone. They no longer accept threats without evidence. They no longer surrender authority out of fear. They stand in calm awareness. Awareness removes the influence of assumption. When assumption loses influence, false authority has no place to stand.

Proof is not an attack. Proof is clarification. Clarification is the natural right of the living. It is the living asking, what is the source of your claim. It is the living asking, who stands behind it. It is the living asking, what agreement was made. If the claimant cannot provide answers, the claim has no substance. A claim without substance cannot bind the living. It exists only in the artificial world. It does not reach the living unless the living accepts it.

The nature of proof begins with understanding that authority must be shown, not assumed. Many people forget this. They see a letter with formal language and assume it carries authority. They see a uniform and assume it carries control. They see a logo and assume it carries legitimacy. These are visual cues. They influence behaviour. They create belief. Belief is not proof. It is perception. Perception can mislead. Proof cannot.

Proof demands that authority be real. Real authority has a clear origin. It can be explained. It can be demonstrated. It does not hide behind vague statements. It does not rely on fear. It does not rely on hurry. It does not ask the living to accept anything without understanding. Real authority stands without pressure. It stands because it is genuine, not because it appears genuine.

Assumed authority is different. It uses appearance. It uses confidence. It uses tone. It uses threat. It uses notice formats designed to look official. It uses urgency to stop people from thinking. It uses fear to stop people from asking questions. It uses behaviour to create the impression of agreement. This type of authority disappears when confronted with a simple request for proof.

The living who requires proof does not challenge for the sake of conflict. They challenge because truth matters. They challenge because clarity protects the living. They challenge because assumption creates silent contracts that the living never intended to enter. Silent contracts are the backbone of modern control. They form when the living obeys without knowing why. Proof stops them from forming.

Proof also reveals intention. When a claimant truly believes in their authority, they welcome the chance to present it. They provide the evidence calmly. They communicate with respect. They understand the request. When a claimant relies on assumption, they avoid proof. They become evasive. They become defensive. They try to shift the conversation back to pressure. They avoid direct questions. They rely on broad statements. They rely on the living giving up before clarity is reached.

This is why the sovereign mind holds firm. It does not surrender when pressure rises. Pressure is not proof. Pressure is a sign of weakness. A claim supported by truth does not require pressure. It stands on merit. Proof reveals this. The living asks, and truth either appears or vanishes. Nothing more is needed.

Understanding the nature of proof also includes recognising that most claims made in the artificial world are automated. Automated systems send notices. Automated systems add charges. Automated systems generate warnings. Automated systems use templates that sound serious but contain nothing personal. These communications appear forceful. They create urgency. But an automated system cannot hold authority over the living. It is not a living being. It cannot consent. It cannot contract. It cannot enforce anything without participation.

When the living asks an automated process for proof, the process fails. It cannot respond. It cannot explain itself. It cannot provide evidence. It was never designed for clarity. It was designed for compliance. The sovereign mind recognises automation instantly and does not allow automation to guide behaviour.

Proof is also tied to identity. A claim must be directed at the correct identity to have any meaning. Many institutions aim claims at the recorded identity. They expect the living to answer for it. The living may choose to represent the recorded identity, but representation is a voluntary act. It cannot be demanded without proof that the recorded identity is bound. When the living asks for proof of the link between the claim and the identity, many claims weaken. Few claimants can explain the distinction. Fewer still can show lawful authority that binds the living. They rely on the living stepping into the role instinctively. Proof prevents this unconscious step.

Requiring proof is a discipline. It is not about arguing. It is not about defeating anyone. It is not about refusing all claims. It is about ensuring that every interaction is based on truth. Truth protects the living. Truth creates boundary. Truth stops fear. Truth prevents manipulation. Truth strengthens dignity. Proof brings truth into the interaction. Without it, the living is vulnerable to influence. With it, the living stands secure.

Proof also slows the process. Many systems rely on urgency. They want the living to react quickly. Reaction-based decision making prevents reflection. Reflection leads to questions. Questions lead to proof. Proof reveals weakness. Weakness dissolves authority. The sovereign mind breaks this chain by slowing down. The living reads slowly. The living speaks slowly. The living decides slowly. Stillness invites clarity. Clarity invites proof. Proof dissolves assumption.

The nature of proof also involves recognising the difference between a claim and truth. A claim is a statement made by someone. It may be true. It may be false. It may be incomplete. It may be misinterpreted. Truth is independent of the claim. Proof connects the two. Without proof, the claim is nothing more than an assertion. Assertions have no inherent authority. The living does not accept assertions. The living accepts truth supported by evidence.

Proof is the foundation of peace. When the living stands on proof, fear vanishes. Fear thrives in uncertainty. Fear grows when the mind imagines consequences. Proof removes uncertainty. Proof replaces imagination with fact. Fact rarely matches fear. Fact is simple. Fear is complex. Proof brings the mind back to reality. Reality is calmer than fear.

The sovereign mind understands that life becomes easier when proof becomes the standard. Decisions become simpler. Boundaries become clearer. Interactions become honest. Authority becomes transparent. The artificial world loses its ability to confuse. Confusion is the tool of assumption. Proof is the antidote.

The nature of proof is the nature of sovereignty. It is the living saying, I choose truth. It is the living saying, show me what stands behind your words. It is the living saying, I do not accept appearance as reality. It is the living saying, I will not act until clarity is present.

The living requires proof. And where proof is absent, the living remains free.

Proof is the point where clarity replaces belief. Most people live in a world shaped by belief rather than evidence. They believe authority exists because they were told it exists. They believe a demand is lawful because it looks official. They believe a process is legitimate because others follow it. They believe they must act because acting has become routine. These beliefs are not based on truth. They are based on conditioning. Conditioning shapes behaviour long before the living learns to question. Proof unravels this conditioning. Proof forces the mind to return to truth rather than habit.

When the living begins to require proof, the artificial world reacts. Systems are comfortable when the living accepts claims silently. Silence helps them. Silence allows assumption to stand. Silence turns suggestion into agreement. Silence allows tone to replace evidence. The moment the living asks a simple question, the structure changes. Systems are designed for compliance. They are not designed for scrutiny. Many claims lose force when examined because their strength was never in truth. Their strength was in the absence of questioning.

The living requires proof because the living values truth more than appearance. Appearance is shallow. It creates impressions. It influences behaviour. People follow appearance because it feels familiar. They accept letters with official formatting because they resemble authority. They answer calls from official sounding voices because those voices sound confident. They obey printed text because they were taught to obey without asking why. These habits allow appearance to act as truth. Proof exposes the difference.

Asking for proof is the moment the living chooses awareness over automatic compliance. Automatic compliance is the strongest tool systems use. It keeps people predictable. It keeps behaviour aligned with expectation. It turns routines into obligations. When people act without thinking, they sign agreements they do not understand. They accept terms they did not examine. They enter implied contracts through silence. Proof breaks this cycle. Proof requires that every claim be understood before any action is taken.

Proof also protects the living from fear-based behaviour. Fear is powerful because it interrupts reason. Fear convinces people that they must act quickly. Fear tells people that hesitation is dangerous. Fear tells people that questioning authority will lead to punishment. These thoughts are not based on truth. They are based on emotion. Systems use fear to prevent questions. Fear stops people from asking for evidence. When the living pauses, the fear weakens. It becomes clear that there is no danger in asking for proof. Asking for proof is a natural right.

The nature of proof also involves understanding the difference between the living and the recorded identity. Many claims are directed at the recorded name. Systems expect the living to respond as the name without thinking. This expectation is based on habit. When the living requires proof that the claim applies to them, the system struggles. The system cannot explain the relationship clearly. It relies on the living acting as the recorded identity without reflection. Proof forces the system to confront its own assumptions. Many cannot.

The living who demands proof does not accept unexplained connections. If a claim is made, the living asks how the claim reaches them. If an obligation is stated, the living asks where it was agreed. If authority is asserted, the living asks for its source. These questions expose the truth. Proof either exists or it does not. If it does not, the claim falls to the ground. If it does exist, the living can examine it and act with clarity. This is not resistance. This is awareness.

Proof is also linked to responsibility. People often forget that responsibility flows in both directions. Systems expect the living to be responsible for their actions. They use this expectation to justify pressure. But claimants also hold responsibility. If a claimant demands something, they must show why. They must explain who they are. They must present evidence. They must answer questions. They cannot shift responsibility onto the living without proof. When the living requires proof, responsibility returns to the claimant. This balance creates fairness.

The sovereign mind understands that authority without proof is nothing more than suggestion. Suggestions can be declined. Suggestions cannot bind the living unless accepted. Many people accept suggestion as law because they never learned to question it. They were trained to obey without evidence. Proof corrects this training. It teaches the living to rely on truth rather than habit. Truth is not afraid of questions. Truth thrives under examination. Truth appears when asked. Assumption does not.

The nature of proof also reveals the structure of false certainty. False certainty is the illusion that a claim is valid simply because it sounds firm. People mistake firm language for lawful basis. They mistake confidence for legitimacy. They mistake formality for authority. Systems rely on this mistake. They craft notices in ways that mimic genuine authority. They use phrases that sound decisive. They format documents to resemble official rulings. These strategies are used to create certainty in the mind of the reader. Proof exposes them. If the claim is real, it can be shown. If the claim is not real, it hides behind formatting.

When the living requires proof, formatting loses impact. The living does not respond to design. The living responds to substance. Substance is shown through evidence. A claim cannot rely on appearance when asked for proof. It must stand on truth. This is why systems become uneasy when proof is requested. They lose control over perception. They must confront reality.

Proof is neutral. It does not take sides. It does not create conflict. It does not support the living or the claimant. Proof reveals what exists. The sovereign mind uses proof as a tool for clarity. It does not use proof to defeat others. It uses proof to understand. Understanding protects the living. Understanding removes fear. Understanding restores dignity.

Proof also shapes boundaries. Boundaries are how the living communicates their limits. Limits must be respected. When someone makes a claim over the living, they are stepping inside the boundary. The living has the right to ask them to step back until the claim is supported. Proof functions as the gateway. If proof is shown, the living considers the claim. If proof is not shown, the living declines the claim. This boundary keeps the living safe from unwanted influence.

The nature of proof is simple. It is the expectation that claims must be true before they can shape the actions of the living. Many people allow claims to shape their behaviour without ever asking whether the claims are real. This surrender removes personal authority. Proof restores it. When the living requires proof, they regain control over their choices. They no longer follow demands blindly. They choose based on truth.

Proof also dismantles the illusion of inevitability. Many systems act as though their demands must be accepted. They create the impression that compliance is the only option. They use deadlines, bold text, and threats to create this impression. But inevitability is an illusion. A claim is not inevitable if it cannot be proven. A demand is not inevitable if it lacks authority. Proof removes the illusion and reveals the interaction for what it is an offer. The living decides whether to accept.

The sovereign mind does not fear proof. It seeks proof. It knows that proof strengthens truth and exposes assumption. It knows that proof protects dignity. It knows that proof defends freedom. It knows that proof must guide every interaction with the artificial world. Systems were designed to rely on assumption. They weaken when faced with clarity.

The nature of proof is the nature of sovereignty. It is the living saying, show me before you expect me to act. It is the living saying, I will not follow without understanding. It is the living saying, truth must stand before authority does. Proof is the barrier that prevents unwanted influence. Proof is the shield that protects the living from assumption. Proof is the tool that restores self-governed thought.

The living requires proof because the living is responsible for their own choices. They do not surrender that responsibility to systems that rely on habit. They do not accept guidance from structures that cannot explain themselves. They do not follow processes that cannot show their origin. The living stands in clarity. The living asks questions. The living waits for evidence. And where evidence does not exist, the living remains free.

Assumption as Authority

Authority in the artificial world survives through assumption. It does not survive through truth. It does not survive through open agreement. It survives because people accept its claims without asking how those claims were formed. This acceptance looks like trust, but it is not trust. It is habit. It is conditioning. It is a pattern taught so early and repeated so often that most people never realise they are following it. Assumption is the fuel that keeps false authority alive.

Assumption works because people believe authority belongs to institutions by default. They believe authority is created by buildings, uniforms, titles, or paperwork. These elements are symbols. Symbols influence behaviour because they have been infused with meaning. But symbols are not authority. Authority must come from truth. Truth must come from evidence. Without evidence, a symbol is nothing more than decoration. A decorated claim is still a claim. It gains power only when the living accepts it without thinking.

Assumption begins with belief. People believe councils have authority in every circumstance. People believe enforcement officers have power because they appear confident. People believe letters from institutions must be obeyed because they look official. People believe certain roles outrank them by nature. None of these beliefs are examined. They exist because society teaches them. When the belief is accepted, the claim is accepted. The claim becomes authority in the mind of the individual, not because it is true, but because it was never questioned.

The living challenges these beliefs. The living does not accept authority that is not shown. The living sees the difference between a claim and truth. A claim must be proven. Truth must be demonstrated. Authority must be explained. When a claim is presented, the living asks, who made it. When authority is asserted, the living asks, on what basis. When terms are suggested, the living asks, where is the agreement. These questions remove assumption. Without assumption, false authority collapses.

Assumption often hides inside language. Institutions use phrases that sound definite. They use terms that suggest power. They write sentences that imply inevitability. They rely on certain words provoking automatic reactions. Words have been used as tools. They guide behaviour. They create the impression of control. They influence without needing clarity. The sovereign mind hears these words differently. It hears them as statements, not truth. It hears them as claims, not authority. It hears them as offers, not orders.

Language can be shaped, but truth cannot. Truth exists separately from language. When authority is real, it can be shown clearly. When authority is assumed, it hides behind strong language. This is why the living asks for proof. Proof forces the claimant to move beyond tone. Tone cannot stand in place of evidence. Strong language cannot substitute for truth. Bold formatting cannot replace lawful basis. When the living removes assumption, these tools lose their power.

Assumption is also built through repetition. People see institutions act in certain ways every day. They see the same letters. They see the same procedures. They see the same behaviours. Over time these actions create familiarity. Familiarity looks like legitimacy. If enough people follow a process, the process appears correct. If enough people obey, obedience appears required. Systems know this. They build routines that create predictable responses. These routines turn assumption into habit.

The sovereign mind does not mistake repetition for truth. It does not accept a claim simply because many people accept it. It does not follow a pattern simply because it has existed for years. It examines every claim individually. It looks for evidence. It looks for clarity. It looks for origin. If proof is absent, the claim does not stand. No amount of repetition can make an unproven claim valid.

Assumption also grows when people confuse authority with confidence. Many claimants act confidently. They speak with certainty. They project power. People often equate this confidence with legitimacy. They assume that someone who appears sure of themselves must know what they are doing. They surrender judgment to the tone of the speaker. This surrender gives false power to those who rely on appearance rather than truth.

The living does not surrender judgment. The living does not measure authority through confidence. Confidence is personal. It does not prove anything. A false claimant can speak with confidence. A genuine claimant can speak quietly. Tone does not change truth. The sovereign mind recognises this. It looks past confidence and seeks evidence. It does not respond to the surface of the interaction. It responds to the substance.

Assumption is also created through lack of clarity. Many systems use vague statements. They avoid specifics. They refer to rules without citing them. They refer to authority without identifying its source. They send notices written in broad terms. Vague communication prevents the living from identifying the actual claim. When the claim cannot be identified, it cannot be questioned. This is how assumption gains strength.

Clarity destroys vagueness. When the living asks for specific proof, vague claims cannot survive. When clarity is required, the claimant must explain themselves. They must speak plainly. They must move away from general statements. They must show evidence. Many cannot. Their authority was never based on proof. It was based on the hope that the living would not ask for clarity.

Assumption also operates through silence. When the living does not question a claim, the system treats the silence as acceptance. Silence is used to build a narrative. The narrative becomes evidence for the system. They say the living did not object. They say the living complied. They say the living accepted the process. None of this is true unless the living gave explicit agreement. Systems rely on the living not challenging this interpretation. Silence becomes a form of non-consent disguised as acceptance.

The sovereign mind does not allow silence to be misinterpreted. It brings clarity into the conversation. It does not react emotionally. It speaks calmly. It asks questions. It makes statements that remove assumption. It does not enter silent contracts. It does not allow others to define its intentions. It controls its own voice. A single sentence asking for proof removes the system's ability to treat silence as acceptance.

Assumption also relies on urgency. Systems often act as though everything must be decided immediately. They create deadlines. They create warnings. They create pressure. Pressure stops people from thinking. It pushes them into quick decisions. Quick decisions are based on emotion rather than clarity. Assumption thrives in speed. Proof thrives in stillness.

The living slows the process down. The living does not accept urgency as a reason to act. Urgency is a tactic. It is used to prevent questions. It is used to prevent examination. It is used to create fear. The sovereign mind does not respond to fear. It responds to clarity. It pauses. It breathes. It waits for understanding. Urgency dissolves under stillness. When urgency dissolves, assumption loses its hold.

The nature of assumption as authority is simple. Authority only stands when the living believes it stands. Assumption creates belief. Belief shapes behaviour. Behaviour creates the appearance of agreement. Agreement looks like consent. Systems rely on this chain. Proof breaks it. When the living requires proof, assumption cannot survive. The claim must stand on evidence. Authority must stand on truth.

The living does not reject all authority. The living rejects unproven authority. The living honours truth. It honours clarity. It honours genuine communication. It does not honour pressure. It does not honour assumption. It does not honour claims built on habit. The sovereign mind accepts only what is real.

Assumption is not removed through aggression. It is removed through awareness. Awareness begins with a simple question. It begins with the living asking, what is the foundation of your claim. This question changes everything. It turns assumed authority into a request. It turns pressure into an offer. It turns fear into clarity.

Assumption loses its power when the living stands in truth. Truth is steady. Truth does not rush. Truth does not fear. Truth does not hide behind tone or formatting. Truth does not require assumption. Truth stands on proof.

The living requires proof. And where assumption replaces proof, the living does not accept the claim.

Assumption is the quiet force that governs modern interactions. It does not shout. It does not demand openly. It does not present clear terms. It works in the background. It shapes behaviour without being seen. It convinces people to accept claims before examining them. It convinces people to follow instructions without knowing their source. It convinces people to obey roles they never agreed to. These actions appear natural because they have become normal. Normality hides assumption. When something becomes normal, people stop questioning it. The sovereign mind sees what others treat as normal and asks whether it is true.

Assumption becomes authority when the living does not recognise that a claim is only a claim. A claim is a statement made by someone. It may reflect truth. It may not. Authority is created only when the living accepts that claim without proof. Acceptance turns a claim into a rule. This transformation happens silently. It happens through behaviour, not agreement. When people act as though a claim is legitimate, it gains strength. The system uses this strength to reinforce itself. Assumption becomes a loop. The more people accept a claim, the stronger it appears. The stronger it appears, the more people accept it.

This loop is broken the moment the living asks for proof. A simple question exposes whether authority exists or whether authority was assumed. If the claimant responds with clarity, the authority may be genuine. If the claimant reacts with pressure or avoidance, the authority was never solid. Many systems prefer avoidance. Avoidance protects the illusion of control. Avoidance keeps the living confused. Confusion is useful. It prevents examination. Examination requires truth. Truth weakens assumption. Systems thrive on unexamined claims.

Assumption also relies on the separation between the living being and the recorded identity. Systems treat the recorded identity as the one bound by obligations. They expect the living to step into that identity whenever addressed. This expectation is so common that most people do not notice it. They assume they must answer as the name. They assume the name and the living are the same. They assume the record defines the living. This assumption gives systems power. It draws the living into roles that were never consciously chosen. When the living requires proof of the link between the recorded identity and the claim, this power weakens. Most claimants cannot explain the relationship. They never expected the question to be asked.

In many cases, assumption is created through formatting. Systems format their notices to look official. They use structured layouts. They use bold text. They use reference numbers. They use technical language. These elements create the impression of authority. People mistake formatting for legitimacy. They see a document that looks serious and assume the claim inside must be lawful. Formatting is not proof. It is presentation. Presentation shapes perception, not truth. Proof must go deeper than appearance. When the living asks for proof, the conversation moves beyond formatting. The claimant must show substance.

Substance is rare when assumption replaces evidence. Many claims rely on repetition rather than truth. They rely on people being familiar with the process. They rely on the idea that if a notice looks like every other notice, the living will respond in the same way as everyone else. Familiarity is powerful because it gives a sense of certainty. Certainty is comforting. Systems use certainty to control behaviour. They create processes that feel predictable. Predictability becomes acceptance. Acceptance becomes assumed authority.

The sovereign mind does not mistake familiarity for truth. It recognises when a process is repeated because it is convenient rather than lawful. It recognises when a pattern exists because no one has questioned it. It recognises when the system uses routine to avoid proof. Routine is not authority. Routine is habit. Habit can be broken in a moment by asking for clarity. A single question weakens a process that has existed for decades. This is the power of awareness.

Assumption gains most of its strength from fear. Fear stops people from questioning. Fear tells people that asking for proof is dangerous. Fear tells them that hesitation will lead to punishment. Fear tells them that authority cannot be challenged. These messages are not based on truth. They are based on conditioning. Fear is learned. It is passed down through generations. People watch others obey and assume they must obey as well. They see compliance everywhere and mistake it for evidence that authority is real. This collective behaviour reinforces assumption. It makes false authority look inevitable.

The sovereign mind does not allow fear to guide choices. It recognises fear as a reaction, not truth. It observes fear without obeying it. When fear is not obeyed, it loses influence. Once fear loses influence, clarity appears. Clarity reveals that asking for proof is not dangerous. It is responsible. It is respectful to oneself. It is necessary. Once the living realises this, assumption falls away. Truth replaces fear. Awareness replaces habit.

Assumption also survives because many people confuse convenience with correctness. They follow instructions because it is easier than questioning them. They respond to notices because that is what they have always done. They obey demands because obedience avoids conflict. They accept authority because resisting feels uncomfortable. Systems rely on this desire for convenience. They create processes that are easier to follow than examine. Examination requires thought. Thought requires time. Time requires intention. Convenience requires nothing. It requires no awareness. It requires no scrutiny. It requires no self-respect. It invites assumption.

The sovereign mind does not choose convenience over truth. It chooses awareness even when awareness requires effort. It does not react to avoid discomfort. It asks for clarity even when clarity takes time. It values truth over speed. It values dignity over convenience. When the living chooses awareness, assumption cannot survive. Assumption relies on the absence of attention. Awareness makes assumption visible. Once visible, assumption loses its power.

Assumption also thrives on the idea that authority is inherent. People believe certain roles automatically outrank them. They believe titles grant power. They believe institutions operate above the living. These beliefs are not based on evidence. They are based on cultural stories. These stories are taught from childhood. They become part of identity. When belief becomes identity, questioning becomes difficult. People feel as though questioning authority is wrong, even if authority cannot be proven. This feeling is the result of conditioning, not truth.

The sovereign mind breaks this conditioning by asking one simple question. What is the source of your authority. This question removes the idea of inherent power. It forces the claimant to explain their foundation. Many cannot. They expected the living to accept their role as superior. They rely on image rather than substance. When the living asks for proof, the claimant must show the origin of their authority. If the origin does not exist, the authority is assumed. The living does not accept assumed authority.

Assumption also uses ambiguity to maintain control. Many statements are written to appear clear at first glance but fall apart when examined. They use language that mixes suggestion with instruction. They use phrasing that can be interpreted in multiple ways. They create the illusion of mandatory terms without ever stating them. This ambiguity benefits the claimant. If challenged, they can say the instruction was only guidance. If followed, they can treat the guidance as consent. Ambiguity allows the system to redefine the interaction based on its own needs. Proof ends ambiguity. Proof requires clear terms. Proof requires direct statements. Proof requires answers that cannot be reshaped later.

The living who requires proof does not allow ambiguity to pass unnoticed. They ask for clarity. They ask for direct statements. They ask for evidence. This removes the system's ability to shift meaning. It forces the claimant to commit to their position. Commitment demands proof. Proof demands truth. Truth exposes assumption.

Assumption holds power only when the living does not see it. Once seen, it loses hold. When the living becomes aware of how assumption works, the artificial world changes shape. Claims that once looked powerful begin to look weak. Language that once sounded forceful becomes empty. Notices that once created fear become ordinary. Processes that once guided behaviour lose influence. This change does not occur because the system changed. It occurs because perception changed. The living stopped accepting assumption as truth.

Assumption survives only when the living participates in it. Participation can be withdrawn. The living withdraws participation by asking for proof. Asking for proof removes assumption. It forces truth into the interaction. Truth cannot be shaped by habit. Truth cannot be shaped by pressure. Truth cannot be shaped by belief. Truth reveals the claim for what it is.

When the living requires proof, assumption is no longer authority. It is exposed as an idea without foundation. Authority returns to its rightful place. Authority begins with the living. Authority stands on truth. Authority does not need assumption. The living does not mistake assumption for reality. The living accepts only what can be proven.

The Hidden Power of Questions

Questions are the strongest tool the living possesses. They do not require force. They do not require conflict. They do not require resistance. They require only awareness. A question changes the balance in any interaction. It stops assumption. It stops momentum. It stops pressure. A question demands clarity. Clarity demands truth. Truth exposes the strength or weakness of the claim. This is why the artificial world prefers silence. Silence allows assumption to spread. A question ends silence.

Most systems expect the living to respond without questioning. They rely on predictable behaviour. They rely on people doing what they always do. They rely on fear guiding decisions. Questions disrupt this pattern. A question slows everything down. It prevents automatic compliance. It forces the claimant to step forward and reveal the source of their claim. Many claimants are not prepared for this. They expect obedience, not dialogue. They expect submission, not inquiry. A question breaks their rhythm.

The power of a question lies in its simplicity. A question does not accuse. It does not attack. It does not provoke. It seeks understanding. Understanding is dangerous to false authority because understanding removes confusion. Confusion hides weakness. Confusion protects assumption. When the living asks a question, confusion disappears. The claimant must answer. If the answer is truthful, the claim stands. If the answer is vague, the claim weakens. If the answer is avoided, the claim collapses.

Questions also reveal intention. A claimant who stands on truth will welcome questions. They will provide clear answers. They will not feel threatened by inquiry because they know their authority has foundation. A claimant who relies on assumption will become uncomfortable. They will shift the conversation. They will avoid direct answers. They will return to pressure. Pressure is the last defence of false authority. It rises when truth cannot. The sovereign mind recognises this pattern instantly.

The hidden power of questions begins with recognising that the living does not need to accept any claim without understanding. Understanding is the starting point of all conscious action. Without understanding, people act on fear or habit. Fear and habit serve the interests of the system. Questions serve the interests of the living. When the living asks for clarity, they reclaim control over the interaction. They decide whether the claim reaches them. They decide whether the claimant has authority. They decide whether the terms align with truth.

Questions expose the difference between authority and confidence. Confidence often disguises weak claims. People mistake a confident tone for legitimacy. They accept statements that sound firm. They comply with demands spoken strongly. Questions remove this illusion. A confident claimant who cannot answer a simple question reveals their weakness. Tone cannot replace truth. When the living uses questions, tone loses influence. Evidence becomes the focus.

There are questions that strike directly at the foundation of any claim. They do not require specialised knowledge. They do not require complex reasoning. They require only presence. Questions such as, who is making the claim. Questions such as, what authority do you rely on. Questions such as, what agreement created this obligation. Questions such as, where is the evidence that binds the living. These questions look simple, but they change everything. They shine a light on areas the claimant hoped to keep in shadow.

Questions also protect the living from invisible contracts. Many obligations are created through behaviour rather than explicit agreement. People follow instructions and unknowingly enter implied terms. Questions prevent this. When the living asks, what am I agreeing to, the implication breaks. When the living asks, what terms are being offered, the process becomes visible. Once visible, implied terms lose power. They require silence to survive. Questions destroy that silence.

The artificial world depends on inertia. It depends on people doing what they have always done. When the living asks questions, they break inertia. They introduce intention where habit once ruled. They bring thought into places where reaction was expected. This change is powerful because it shifts authority back to the living. The claimant can no longer carry the interaction alone. They must respond. They must show themselves. They must become accountable.

Questions also slow down the pace of pressure. Pressure works by speed. It encourages quick decisions. It discourages reflection. It aims to overwhelm the mind. A question stops this. It interrupts the process. It creates a pause. The pause allows the living to regain control of their thoughts. It allows them to breathe. It allows them to see the situation clearly. Pressure loses its force when the living is calm. Questions create calm.

Questions also reveal relationship. Many claimants assume a superior position. They act as though they stand above the living. They rely on this perceived hierarchy to gain compliance. A question removes the hierarchy. It places both individuals on equal ground. It transforms the interaction into an exchange. Exchanges require mutual respect. False authority hates equality. It thrives only when the living forgets their own power.

The hidden power of questions comes from the fact that they require nothing in return. A question needs no approval. A question needs no permission. A question is not an act of defiance. It is a request for truth. Even false authority cannot deny the legitimacy of asking. When a claimant refuses to answer, they reveal their position. When they evade, they expose their intent. When they respond with aggression, they demonstrate their lack of foundation.

Questions also remove emotional influence. When confronted with a demand, many people feel fear or anger. These emotions cloud judgment. They create urgency. They push people into reactions. Questions restore rational thinking. The moment a question is asked, emotion diminishes. The mind shifts from reaction to investigation. Investigation is calm. Calmness is power. Calmness reveals truth more effectively than confrontation.

The living uses questions to protect dignity. Dignity comes from standing in truth. It comes from refusing to act blindly. It comes from valuing oneself enough to require understanding. When the living asks questions, they communicate that they will not accept anything without clarity. This is not disrespect. It is self-respect. It is honouring the boundary between the living and the artificial world.

Questions also reveal the depth of a claim. A weak claim collapses under one or two questions. A stronger claim may survive longer. A genuine claim will stand easily. The living can gauge the truth by the strength of the answers. If answers require more questions, the claim was not clear. If answers contradict each other, the claim was not genuine. If answers avoid the original question, the claimant is unsure. This method reveals truth without aggression.

Questions weaken intimidation. Intimidation relies on silence. It relies on the living feeling small. It relies on the belief that questioning authority is dangerous. When the living speaks calmly, intimidation dissolves. A question signals that the living is not overwhelmed. It signals clarity. It signals strength. The more calmly the question is asked, the faster intimidation disappears.

Systems rely on compliance. Compliance collapses when questions appear. A process that expects obedience struggles when clarity is required. A letter designed to look official becomes an offer when questioned. A demand becomes a request. A threat becomes an empty sentence. Questions change the meaning of everything. They reveal the true nature of the interaction.

Questions also prevent escalation. When the living reacts emotionally, escalation follows. When the living asks a question, the tone stays calm. The claimant must respond to the question, not to emotion. This keeps the interaction grounded. It removes the need for conflict. It allows truth to surface naturally. A calm interaction benefits the living. It exposes the claimant. It protects dignity.

The hidden power of questions is the power to remove illusion. Illusion keeps systems functioning. It convinces people that authority is unquestionable. It convinces them that refusal is impossible. It convinces them that clarity is irrelevant. Questions shatter illusions. They bring light into places where confusion was used to create control.

When the living asks questions, the artificial world must reveal its structure. Most of that structure is weaker than it appears. Authority borrowed from assumption collapses when asked to explain itself. Authority taken through habit returns to nothing when examined. Authority created through tone looks empty when questioned. True authority does not fear questions.

The living carries this power always. A question weighs nothing. It costs nothing. It requires no preparation. It requires only awareness. Awareness is the root of sovereignty. Awareness turns the living into the author of their own path.

The living asks. The claimant must answer. In that moment, the balance shifts. Truth becomes visible. False authority becomes exposed. The living remains free.

Questions are the doorway to truth. They open the space where clarity can enter. Without questions, every interaction becomes a one-sided flow of claims, demands, and expectations. Questions stop that flow. They create balance. They give the living a voice. They turn a monologue into a dialogue. Dialogue forces the claimant to step into the light. That moment is where truth becomes visible.

Many people do not ask questions because they do not believe they are allowed to. They think authority must not be questioned. They think questioning will lead to consequences. They think their role is to obey. These thoughts come from conditioning. Conditioning teaches people that authority sits above them. Conditioning teaches people that instructions must be followed without hesitation. Conditioning teaches people that the correct response to a demand is compliance. None of this is truth. These are beliefs created through repetition.

The sovereign mind breaks these beliefs by asking one question. A single question creates a crack in the structure of assumed authority. Once the crack appears, more questions follow naturally. The living begins to see that nothing collapses when they speak. Nothing dangerous happens when they seek clarity. Nothing bad happens when they require proof. The world does not end when the living asks, what is the basis of your claim. It is the beginning of their presence returning.

Questions reveal the limits of the claimant. The artificial world creates the illusion that claimants have complete control. It uses procedures. It uses scripts. It uses designed processes. It uses tone. But these tools are not limitless. They are fragile. They depend on the living accepting the performance as reality. A question disrupts the performance. When the living asks for clarity, the claimant must move beyond the script. Scripted authority collapses when forced to operate outside its routine.

Questions also reveal intent. Some claimants act with genuine belief in their authority. They may still be mistaken, but they are not acting with malice. When questioned, they attempt to answer honestly. Their honesty shows sincerity, even if their understanding is limited. Other claimants know their authority is assumed. They rely on tone and confidence to create the appearance of legitimacy. When questioned, they deflect. They repeat the same lines. They avoid the centre of the question. This avoidance reveals the weakness of their position.

The sovereign mind recognises these differences. It does not attack honesty. It does not become aggressive toward uncertainty. It remains calm. It continues asking simple, direct questions. Calm questions create a stable space where truth has no choice but to appear. If truth is present, the claimant will provide it. If truth is absent, the claimant will expose themselves through avoidance.

Questions also protect the living from internal assumptions. People often assume they know what a notice means. They assume the consequences are real. They assume the terms are mandatory. They assume the claimant has authority. These assumptions are internal, not external. They arise from fear, habit, or misunderstanding. Questions break internal assumptions by forcing the mind to move from belief to investigation. Investigation weakens imagination. Imagination fuels fear. When imagination is replaced with truth, fear fades.

A notice stating that action will be taken means nothing until the living asks, what action and by what authority. A letter stating that payment is due means nothing until the living asks, what agreement created this obligation. A claimant who asserts authority speaks only words until the living asks, what is the source of your authority. These questions move from assumption to clarity. Clarity changes the entire dynamic.

Questions also protect against emotional pressure. Many claimants rely on tone to create urgency. They hope to overwhelm the living. They hope the living will act from fear. Fear creates quick decisions. Quick decisions create silent contracts. Silent contracts give systems control. Questions break emotional pressure. The moment the living asks a calm question, the emotional energy collapses. The conversation shifts from emotion to logic. Logic favours the living because logic seeks truth.

It is important to understand that questions are not resistance. They are the natural language of awareness. Resistance creates conflict. Questions create understanding. Conflict invites escalation. Understanding invites truth. The sovereign mind uses questions because they are steady. They are grounded. They do not create unnecessary tension. They create clarity without confrontation.

Questions also demonstrate presence. Presence means the living is fully aware of themselves and the interaction. Systems rely on people being mentally absent. They hope the living will follow patterns automatically. When the living asks a question, it signals that they are present. Presence disrupts assumption. Presence shows the claimant that they are being watched, heard, and evaluated. Many claimants are unprepared for this. They expect compliance, not presence.

Presence also brings the living into their own authority. Authority begins with awareness. When the living is present, they do not react based on fear or conditioning. They respond based on truth. Truth is calm. Truth is steady. Truth is not afraid of questions. The living asks from truth. The claimant must answer from truth or reveal their lack of it.

Questions also help the living understand the scope of the claim. Many claims are broad. They suggest wide authority. They suggest unavoidable obligations. They suggest power that reaches beyond its real limits. When the living asks specific questions, the claim becomes smaller. Boundaries become visible. The claimant must define their limits. Defined limits reduce fear. Undefined authority appears large and overwhelming. Defined authority appears limited and manageable. Questions create definition.

The hidden power of questions is that they shift responsibility. When a claimant makes a statement, responsibility rests with them. They must justify what they say. They must support their words. They must provide evidence. Many claimants try to shift responsibility to the living. They say the living must comply. They say the living must provide information. They say the living must act. Questions reverse this. They place responsibility back on the claimant. The claimant must answer. The claimant must support their claim. The claimant must show clarity.

Questions also shape boundaries. Boundaries are essential to sovereignty. Without boundaries, the living is vulnerable to external influence. Questions defend boundaries by preventing unclear claims from entering. They force the claimant to approach the boundary openly. If the claimant cannot cross with truth, they cannot cross at all. The boundary holds. The living remains protected.

Many people believe they must have complex knowledge to challenge authority. This is false. Knowledge is not required. Awareness is required. Awareness expresses itself through questions. A simple question is more effective than a page of information. Information can be argued. Questions cannot. A question is either answered or avoided. Avoidance is evidence. Evidence reveals truth.

Questions expose contradictions. When a claimant makes inconsistent statements, the inconsistencies become visible through questioning. Contradictions reveal confusion. Confusion reveals weakness. Weakness reveals assumption. The sovereign mind does not attack contradictions. It simply observes them. The claimant exposes themselves. The living remains calm.

Questions also prevent escalation from becoming personal. When the interaction stays focused on the claim, not the individual, emotions stay balanced. The claimant cannot accuse the living of being unreasonable when the living is calmly asking for clarity. The claimant cannot frame the living as hostile when the living is seeking truth. Questions protect dignity.

The hidden power of questions is not in their complexity. It is in their sincerity. A sincere question holds more strength than a thousand assumptions. It requires presence. It requires calm. It requires clarity. These qualities form the foundation of sovereignty.

When the living asks questions, they reclaim their place. They step out of confusion. They step out of fear. They step out of assumption. They step into truth.

Questions bring the living back to themselves. They bring the claimant back to truth. They bring the interaction back to balance. Authority must face scrutiny. Scrutiny begins with a question.

A question weighs nothing, yet it carries the full power of awareness. It is the tool that reveals truth without force. It is the tool that dissolves assumption without conflict. It is the tool that keeps the living free.

The living asks, and the artificial world must answer. In that moment, authority is tested. Truth becomes visible. The living stands steady.

And the one who stands steady cannot be controlled.

Paper Does Not Equal Truth

Paper is one of the strongest tools used by the artificial world. It carries symbols. It carries formatting. It carries titles and numbers. It carries language designed to create certainty. People see paper and assume authority. They see printed words and assume truth. They see structured layouts and assume legitimacy. These reactions come from conditioning. Conditioning teaches the living to treat paper as unquestionable. But paper is not truth. Paper is only paper. It is a medium for words. It is not evidence of authority. It is not proof of agreement. It is not a contract unless the living consciously accepts it.

The artificial world relies heavily on paper because paper creates the illusion of certainty. A notice that arrives through the door feels serious. A document with bold headings appears official. A letter using formal language appears lawful. The mind interprets these signals quickly. People react before they think. They assume the content has power because the presentation looks familiar. Familiarity shapes emotion. Emotion shapes behaviour. This is how paper becomes a tool of control without containing any real authority.

The living must separate appearance from truth. Appearance is created through design. Truth is revealed through evidence. A perfectly formatted notice can contain no lawful basis. A poorly formatted note can contain truth. Authority is not created by a header. Authority is not created by a stamp. Authority is not created by the shape of the page. Authority must come from a clear source. If the source cannot be shown, the document is meaningless. It carries no weight over the living.

Paper also gains influence through repetition. People see similar documents throughout their lives. Bills, forms, notices, warnings, demands, statements. Over time these documents create behavioural patterns. People respond instantly because they have responded instantly for years. They pay without thinking. They comply without questioning. They accept terms without reading. This repetition turns paper into an unspoken instruction. Instructions become obligations. Obligations become assumed authority. This transformation happens through routine, not truth.

The sovereign mind breaks routine by looking past the formatting. It asks, what is the claim. It asks, who is making it. It asks, what evidence supports it. These questions remove the influence of presentation. Presentation becomes irrelevant when substance is examined. Many documents contain strong language but weak claims. Many contain demands but no evidence. Many contain instructions but no authority. When the living seeks truth, the surface loses power.

Paper also influences behaviour because people fear the consequences suggested within it. They read the words will be taken or must be paid and assume danger. They imagine outcomes that have not been proven. They respond to these imagined outcomes rather than to the truth of the claim. Paper does not create consequences. Paper describes statements. A statement is only a claim. Claims must be proven. The living does not act on claims that are not supported.

The artificial world uses paper to create the appearance of control. Yet most paper relies on assumptions rather than truth. Many notices imply obligations without stating their source. They hint at authority without providing evidence. They reference procedures without explaining their foundation. These documents survive because the living rarely asks for proof. The moment proof is required, the document must stand on something real. Many cannot.

Paper also attempts to bind the recorded identity to the claim. It uses the name. It uses reference numbers. It uses phrases that suggest obligation. But the recorded identity is not the living being. It is an administrative construct. A document directed at the recorded identity must show evidence that the living is bound. If the claimant cannot show this, the paper has no connection to the living. The connection must be proven. It cannot be assumed. Many documents rely on people stepping into the recorded identity automatically. Awareness prevents this automatic step.

The living understands that paper without proof is nothing more than suggestion. Suggestions can be declined. They do not control the living unless the living accepts them. Acceptance can be intentional or unintentional. Unintentional acceptance happens when the living reacts emotionally, pays quickly, or complies without thought. Intentional acceptance happens only when the living sees truth in the claim. Truth is revealed through evidence, not through presentation.

Paper often acts as an intermediary for automated systems. Automated letters are generated by algorithms. They are not written by a living being who understands the situation. They contain generic phrases. They contain standard warnings. They contain automatic language that does not apply to the specific living being. Automation cannot hold authority. Authority must come from a living source that can explain itself. When the living asks for proof, automation cannot answer. It was never designed to.

Paper also relies on the belief that receiving a document means entering a process. Receiving a letter does not create obligation. Receiving a notice does not create agreement. Receiving instructions does not create a contract. The living must consciously choose to participate. The artificial world tries to blur this distinction. It treats delivery of a document as acceptance of the terms. This is an illusion. Acceptance requires intention. Intention must come from the living. Paper cannot create intention.

The sovereign mind remains calm when paper arrives. It does not react. It observes. It reads slowly. It separates language from truth. It asks questions. It seeks clarity. It looks for the source. It measures the claim. It requests proof. This calm approach removes the emotional impact created by formatting. When emotion is removed, the document loses its power. It becomes what it always was, a piece of paper containing words.

Paper often makes claims sound absolute. It uses phrases such as you must or action will be taken. These phrases are designed to create fear. Fear leads to compliance. Fear bypasses thought. Yet the phrases themselves are only words. They do not create authority. Authority must be demonstrated separately. If the claimant cannot show the basis for the threat, the threat is empty. Empty threats appear strong only when accepted without thought.

The living knows that paper cannot harm them. Paper cannot enter their home. Paper cannot make decisions for them. Paper cannot bind them without consent. Paper cannot override the truth of the living. It can request. It can suggest. It can attempt to influence. But it cannot control. Control must be given, not taken. The living does not give control to paper.

Documents also attempt to use deadlines to create urgency. Urgency manipulates the mind. It encourages quick actions. It discourages questions. It prevents calmness. When the living sees a deadline, they do not rush. They ask for proof. If proof cannot be provided, the deadline has no meaning. A demand without authority cannot impose time. Time becomes relevant only when the claim is valid. Until then, the document remains an offer.

The artificial world values compliance. Compliance is easier to maintain when people believe paper is truth. But compliance is fragile. It relies on unexamined behaviour. Once the living examines the claim, the structure collapses. Most documents cannot stand under scrutiny. They survive only when people choose not to question them. When the living asks, the truth appears. The truth is often simpler than the document suggests.

Paper has authority only when the living believes it does. Belief is not truth. Belief is habit. Truth is evidence. When the living requires evidence, the belief fades. The claim must stand on its own foundation. If the foundation is weak, the claim is weak. If the foundation is absent, the claim is nothing.

The sovereign mind recognises paper as a tool, not as truth. It treats documents as statements made by a claimant. It does not treat them as orders. It does not treat them as proof. It does not treat them as binding. It evaluates them. It examines them. It questions them. This approach removes the illusion of control that paper tries to project.

Paper does not equal truth. Truth stands without paper. Truth stands without formatting. Truth stands without strong language. Truth stands without fear. Truth can be shown clearly. Truth does not hide behind presentation. When the living looks beyond the page, the actual claim appears. When the claim appears, proof becomes the only standard.

The living accepts only what is true. The living accepts only what can be proven. The living does not surrender authority to paper. The living stands in clarity. The living sees through appearance. The living requires evidence.

And where evidence is absent, the document holds no power.

Paper gains power only when the living forgets its true nature. It is an object. It holds ink. It carries marks. It communicates ideas. But it has no life. It has no force. It has no authority by itself. It is a carrier of claims, not the source of them. When the living remembers this, paper loses its ability to intimidate. When the living forgets, paper becomes a tool for those who rely on appearance rather than truth.

People often feel tension when receiving a formal document. The tension does not come from the paper. It comes from the ideas attached to it. These ideas were learned over time. Paper has been used to mark grades in school. Paper has been used to issue instructions. Paper has been used to demand payments. Paper has been used to grant approvals. Paper has been used to deny requests. All of this creates a psychological link. The mind associates paper with judgment. Judgment becomes fear. Fear becomes compliance.

The sovereign mind breaks this link by treating paper as neutral. The living reads the content without giving it more weight than it deserves. It does not accept the emotional impact. It focuses on the claim. The claim must stand independently of the paper. If a claim is not strong enough to stand on its own, it should not influence the living. Many documents contain large words but small truth. They depend on the reader reacting emotionally. Emotional reactions block clarity. Clarity requires calm. When the living remains calm, the paper loses its power.

Paper also carries the authority of the organisation that created it. Organisations rely on their image. They expect their logo to influence behaviour. They expect their letterhead to create compliance. They expect their structure to appear imposing. But a symbol printed on a page is not authority. Authority must be shown. Authority must have origin. Authority must be connected to truth. A symbol is not a source. It is a mark. Marks do not control the living unless the living accepts them.

Systems know that paper creates the impression of distance. Distance weakens the confidence of the reader. The paper arrives without a face. It arrives without a voice. It arrives without context. Many people accept the claim because they do not know who stands behind it. A name printed on a page is not a living claimant. It is a representation. Representations must be supported by evidence. The living has the right to know who is making the claim. If the claimant cannot be identified, the claim has no weight.

Paper uses language to create authority. This language is carefully designed. It uses short sentences that sound absolute. It uses phrases that suggest consequences. It uses words that create urgency. It uses structure that limits the reader's options. These techniques aim to shape behaviour without providing proof. They rely on emotion. They do not rely on truth. When the living reads carefully, the techniques become visible. Visibility removes influence. Influence thrives in confusion, not clarity.

Paper often presents terms as though they cannot be questioned. It suggests compliance is required. It suggests agreement has already been made. It suggests the living is already bound. These suggestions are not truth. They are attempts to lead the reader. The living recognises that a suggestion is not an obligation. The living asks, what agreement do these terms rely on. If no agreement exists, the terms do not apply. Paper cannot create obligations by declaring them. Obligations must be chosen by the living. Choice cannot be taken through ink.

Many documents assume that the living will not ask for proof. They are written with the expectation of compliance. They rely on the reader not questioning the foundation of the claim. When the living asks for proof, the structure becomes unstable. Documents that appear solid become weak under examination. Questions expose gaps. Questions expose contradictions. Questions expose missing evidence. These gaps reveal that many documents are based on assumption rather than authority.

Paper also attempts to create fear through references to processes. It says the account will be passed on. It says further action will follow. It says escalation may occur. These phrases are intentionally vague. They imply danger without specifying it. The mind fills the gap with imagination. Imagination creates fear. Fear creates compliance. When the living asks, what is this process and who controls it, the illusion collapses. Most of these statements are general. They are not tied to any specific truth. They exist to influence.

The sovereign mind recognises this pattern. It knows that fear thrives in uncertainty. It removes uncertainty by requiring clarity. It removes imagination by asking for proof. It replaces emotion with awareness. Awareness makes fear unnecessary. The living does not react to threats that lack evidence. Threats without evidence are empty. Empty threats dissolve when questioned.

Paper often arrives in a sequence. The sequence creates a story. The story suggests that each step increases seriousness. The reader begins to believe the process is progressing. This belief is created through repetition. One letter follows another. Each letter sounds more urgent. But urgency does not create authority. Urgency is a tool. It is often used when truth is weak. The living does not allow a sequence of paper to shape their understanding. They treat each document separately. Each claim must be proven. A history of unproven claims does not create a valid one.

Paper also tries to impose identity. It uses the recorded name to direct the claim. It treats the name as the living being. The living knows this is not true. The recorded identity is an administrative label. It is not the living. When the living requires proof that the claim applies to them, the gap becomes clear. Many claimants cannot explain the link between the paper and the living. They rely on habit. Habit is not authority. Habit is not truth. Habit can be broken with awareness.

The living who sees paper as merely paper does not feel the pressure others feel. They do not absorb the emotional weight of the document. They see it as a statement made by someone. They treat it as an offer. They evaluate the offer. They examine the claim. They ask for proof. This simple approach transforms the interaction. Paper cannot intimidate someone who treats it as neutral. Intimidation requires belief. Belief requires conditioning. Conditioning loses its power when the living steps into awareness.

Paper cannot force consent. Consent must come from the living. Consent must be intentional. Consent must be clear. Many documents attempt to use silence as consent. They say your failure to respond will be taken as acceptance. This is not truth. Silence does not create agreement. Agreement requires action. A claimant cannot manufacture agreement through wording. The living recognises this. The living does not accept attempts to create obligation through silence. Silence is not consent. Silence is not agreement. Silence does not bind the living.

Paper attempts to create the illusion that the situation is already decided. This illusion removes the idea of choice. But the living always has choice. The living cannot be bound by wording alone. The living chooses their own path. The living decides which claims they accept. The living decides which terms they agree to. A document cannot remove this freedom. It can only influence behaviour. Influence works only when the living is unaware of it. Awareness dissolves influence.

When the living reads a document, they do not ask, what must I do. They ask, what is being claimed. They ask, who is making the claim. They ask, where is the proof. These questions remove the emotional energy of the paper. They turn the moment from reaction to understanding. Understanding is the beginning of sovereignty.

Paper does not equal truth. Truth stands outside of paper. Truth stands without formatting. Truth is supported by evidence, not by design. When the living looks beyond the layout, the words lose their effect. When the living asks for proof, the claim must stand or fall. Many fall. The artificial world depends on people reacting to appearance. The sovereign mind responds only to truth.

The living does not grant authority to paper. The living grants authority only to truth. Truth must be proven. Truth must be clear. Truth must stand without assumption.

Paper cannot create truth. Paper can only carry statements. Statements must be examined. Proof must be required. The living must remain calm.

Where proof is absent, paper has no power.

Understanding the Claimant

A claim is only as strong as the one who makes it. The artificial world teaches people to focus on the document or the demand, not the claimant behind it. This is by design. When people focus on the paper, they forget to question the source. When they forget the source, they forget the limits. They forget that every notice, every demand, every instruction, and every assertion begins with a living being or a process created by one. If the living does not know who stands behind the claim, they cannot understand the claim itself.

Understanding the claimant is central to sovereignty. Authority does not exist in isolation. Authority comes from someone. The identity of that someone matters. Their role matters. Their limits matter. Their understanding matters. A claim is not valid because it is written. A claim is valid only when the claimant can stand behind it with truth. Many claimants rely on anonymity. They hide behind titles. They hide behind the name of an organisation. They hide behind scripted statements. These layers create distance. Distance prevents questioning. Distance creates fear. Fear creates compliance.

When the living asks, who is making the claim, the distance collapses. The claimant must step forward. They must speak. They must show that they are real. They must identify themselves as the one responsible for the words. This is where most artificial authority weakens. Many claimants cannot speak clearly about their own authority. They were trained to follow procedures, not to understand them. They rely on routines created by others. They rely on systems that operate without transparency. Once they are asked to explain themselves, the illusion begins to break.

Understanding the claimant begins with recognising that institutions are not alive. They do not think. They do not act. They do not hold opinions. They do not make claims. Living people within those institutions do. A notice from an organisation is not a notice from an entity with independent authority. It is a notice produced by a process controlled by someone. That someone carries responsibility. They may try to hide behind the institution's identity, but the institution cannot speak. Only people can. The living has the right to know which person has made the claim.

Many claimants avoid identifying themselves because they do not want to be accountable. Accountability requires clarity. Clarity requires truth. Truth exposes the limits of their authority. An unidentified claimant relies on the recipient feeling small. They rely on the recipient feeling powerless. They rely on the recipient accepting the claim without understanding who stands behind it. When the living asks for identity, this imbalance disappears.

A claimant must be able to explain the nature of their authority. Authority must have an origin. It must have a foundation. It must have a scope. It must have limits. Many claimants do not understand their own authority. They were trained in tasks, not truth. They follow guidelines. They follow instructions. They follow scripts. They believe the structure defines authority. They do not realise that authority must be proven, not performed. When the living asks for the source of authority, the claimant must move beyond performance. They must move into truth. This is where most claims weaken.

Understanding the claimant also involves recognising the difference between someone acting in a role and someone acting as the living. A role is not a person. A role is a function. It is a set of instructions. It is a position created by an institution. Many claimants speak from the role. They repeat official lines. They rely on institutional phrases. They hide behind the title. But a role cannot carry authority unless the living behind it can prove that authority. The living behind the role is the true claimant. The role is a mask. When the living asks, who are you beneath the role, the mask loses its force.

The sovereign mind looks behind the mask. It does not accept claims from titles. Titles are adopted. Titles are assigned. Titles do not create truth. Only a living being can stand in truth. A living being must show evidence. A living being must answer questions. A living being must demonstrate that the claim they make has substance. This requirement separates genuine authority from assumed authority.

Understanding the claimant includes identifying whether they are acting from knowledge or from assumption. Many claimants act from assumption. They assume their role gives them power. They assume their institution supports them fully. They assume their script reflects truth. They assume the living will comply. When the living asks simple questions, these assumptions are exposed. A claimant who acts from assumption will struggle to respond. They will return to script. They will repeat rehearsed lines. They will avoid direct answers. These behaviours reveal their position clearly.

A claimant acting from knowledge behaves differently. They do not avoid questions. They do not become defensive. They do not rely on tone. They provide clear evidence. They explain their authority calmly. They understand the structure they represent. They are aware of their limits. This type of claimant is rare. The artificial world prefers assumption because assumption is easy to maintain. Knowledge requires understanding. Understanding requires accountability. Accountability limits the system.

Understanding the claimant also removes the emotional impact of a claim. People often react emotionally because they imagine authority as something large and powerful. They imagine institutions as towering structures. They imagine claimants as agents of unstoppable force. This imagination is created by distance and anonymity. When the living identifies the claimant, the imagination dissolves. The claimant becomes human. Humans have limits. Humans make mistakes. Humans can be questioned. Humans must provide proof. Once the claimant is seen as human, fear fades. Fear requires distance. Awareness removes distance.

Many claimants expect compliance because they rarely face questions. They operate in environments where people do not challenge them. They become accustomed to authority being assumed. When the living asks for proof, the claimant realises they cannot rely on routine. This realisation often creates hesitation. Hesitation exposes weakness. Weakness exposes assumption. Assumption cannot survive under scrutiny. The sovereign mind uses questions to bring the claimant into clarity.

Understanding the claimant also involves recognising that many claims are made by automated systems. Automation cannot hold authority. Automation cannot answer questions. Automation cannot explain the origin of its claims. Automation creates the appearance of activity. It generates letters. It sends notices. It escalates processes. But it does not understand truth. It does not understand agreement. It does not understand consent. When the living asks for proof, automation fails instantly. It must be replaced by a living claimant. This transition exposes the structure behind the process.

Automation thrives when the living behaves automatically. Awareness stops automation. When the living requires a living claimant to step forward, automation loses its power. A process cannot control the living. Only a living being can attempt to make a claim. That living being must identify themselves. They must take responsibility for the words. They must provide evidence. Many cannot. This is why artificial systems prefer automation. Automation avoids accountability. Accountability is dangerous to false authority.

Understanding the claimant also prevents the living from being misled by tone. Many claimants use firm tone to project authority. Tone is not proof. Tone is performance. Tone influences emotion, not truth. When the living understands the claimant, tone becomes irrelevant. The living listens to substance. Substance must come from evidence. Evidence must come from truth. Truth is not shaped by tone.

Understanding the claimant weakens intimidation. Intimidation works only when the living believes they are being addressed by a powerful force. When the claimant is identified as a person repeating a procedure, intimidation dissolves. The living sees that there is no force behind the words. There is only a claim. A claim must be proven. Intimidation cannot replace proof.

Understanding the claimant also reveals when authority is genuine. Some claims are legitimate. Some claimants speak from real duty. Some have limits defined by truth. When the living asks questions, genuine authority becomes clear through consistency and evidence. The sovereign mind does not reject genuine authority. The sovereign mind rejects only false authority. Questions create the distinction.

The living understands that every claim comes from someone. That someone must step into the light. They must show who they are. They must show why they speak. They must show how their words apply to the living. Without this clarity, the claim holds no power.

Understanding the claimant is understanding the claim. The two cannot be separated. A claim without a claimant is an illusion. A claimant without truth is assumption. The living accepts neither illusion nor assumption.

The living accepts only what is true. The living accepts only what is proven. The living accepts only what is presented openly by a claimant who stands behind their words with evidence.

Where the claimant cannot be identified, the claim falls.

Where the claimant cannot provide proof, the claim dissolves.

Where the claimant hides behind structure, the living does not follow.

The living requires truth.

The living requires clarity.

The living requires proof.

To understand the claimant is to understand the truth behind the claim. A claim does not exist on its own. It cannot float in the air. It cannot enforce itself. It cannot stand without a source. Every claim must begin with someone who asserts it. That someone must hold responsibility for the words, for the intention, and for the expectations placed on the living. When the living identifies the claimant, the structure of the interaction becomes visible. When the claimant remains hidden, the structure becomes a fog where assumption replaces clarity.

Many systems hide the claimant on purpose. This is not an accident. It is a method. It is a design choice. When a claim arrives without a clearly identified human source, the living cannot address it directly. They cannot ask questions. They cannot establish accountability. They cannot seek clarity. They are left with only the paper or the notice. The notice then appears to stand as authority. But the notice is not alive. It is not responsible. It cannot answer questions. It cannot hold truth. It can only create pressure.

Understanding the claimant removes this illusion. When the living asks, who is making this claim, they shift the dynamic. The responsibility moves from the paper to the person. The person must stand behind the claim. They must show their authority. They must provide proof. They must show that the living is bound. Many claimants cannot do this. They were trained to speak on behalf of an institution, not on behalf of truth. When the institution is questioned, the claimant often steps back. They may refer to policy instead of evidence. They may refer to procedure instead of lawful basis. They may repeat phrases without understanding them. These responses reveal that the authority they rely on is not grounded.

Understanding the claimant also requires recognising the difference between a claimant acting in good faith and a claimant acting through pressure. A claimant acting in good faith may still be limited by their own misunderstanding. They may believe in the process. They may think their role grants them authority. They may assume the structure is lawful because they were never taught to question it. These claimants are not deceptive. They are unaware. Their answers will reflect this. They will attempt to explain, but their explanations will lack substance. This shows the structural weakness, not personal malice.

A claimant acting through pressure behaves differently. They avoid questions. They become defensive. They rely on tone. They escalate the situation. They shift responsibility back onto the living. They use phrases that sound serious but lack clarity. They attempt to intimidate. These behaviours show that the claimant is aware of the weakness in their position. They know they cannot prove the claim. They hope the living will surrender under pressure. When the living remains calm, the pressure loses force. The weakness becomes visible. The claimant reveals themselves through their behaviour.

Understanding the claimant also shows the role of hierarchy in the artificial world. Many claimants assume authority because of the position they inhabit. They treat the role as a shield. They believe the role gives them power. But power without foundation is not authority. A role is not evidence. A role is a title. Titles are created by institutions. Institutions are created by living beings. No title can rise above the living. No title can override truth. No title can bind the living without proof.

A claimant who acts as the role rather than as themselves does not understand authority. They assume they have power simply because they occupy a position. When the living asks for proof of authority, the claimant must step out of the role and speak as a human being. This moment often reveals confusion. The claimant realises they cannot depend on the role alone. They must show the origin of their power. Many cannot. They were taught to enforce procedures, not to understand them.

The sovereign mind knows that authority begins with the living. It does not begin with roles. It does not begin with institutions. It does not begin with documents. Authority must be proven. It must be based on truth. It must be supported by evidence. When the living asks for the origin of authority, the claimant's understanding is tested. If the claimant cannot explain the basis of their claim, they cannot enforce it. A claim that cannot be explained cannot bind the living.

Understanding the claimant also reveals the importance of intent. The artificial world hides intent behind formal language. It claims to act on behalf of systems, not individuals. But systems do not have intent. Systems are constructs. Processes do not have intent. Processes are sequences. Only living beings have intent. When a living being makes a claim, their intention matters. If their intention is to intimidate, the behaviour shows it. If their intention is to follow a routine blindly, their answers show it. If their intention is to uphold truth, the evidence supports it. Intent becomes clear when the claimant is brought into the light.

The sovereign mind does not assume intent. It observes behaviour. It watches how the claimant responds when asked to provide clarity. A claimant who responds calmly and openly may hold genuine belief in their authority. A claimant who responds with fear or aggression reveals the lack of foundation. Aggression is a sign of insecurity. Insecurity is a sign of weak authority. Weak authority cannot bind the living.

Understanding the claimant also requires the living to recognise that many claims are generated by systems rather than individuals. Automated claims come from software, not from humans. These claims are the weakest of all. Software cannot hold authority. Software cannot stand behind a claim. Software does not understand the truth. It does not understand consent. It does not understand obligation. It simply follows instructions written by someone else. When the living asks for proof, automation collapses. It must be replaced by a living claimant. That claimant must show authority. They often struggle to explain the system they represent because they did not design it.

When automation is exposed, the artificial world loses force. Automation thrives when the living behaves automatically. Awareness stops automation. Awareness requires the claimant to step forward. Once a living claimant steps forward, accountability appears. Accountability is the foundation of truth. Truth is the foundation of authority. Anything that cannot survive accountability is false authority.

Understanding the claimant also requires the living to examine whether the claimant has personal knowledge of the matter. Many claimants act without understanding the details. They follow instructions blindly. They rely on templates. They rely on scripts. They rely on internal guidelines that do not reflect truth. When the living asks specific questions, the claimant's lack of knowledge becomes visible. This lack of knowledge reveals the thinness of the authority they attempt to project.

A claimant who does not understand the claim cannot prove it. They can only repeat it. Repetition is not evidence. Repetition is habit. Habits cannot bind the living. Only truth can. When the living requires proof, the repeated words lose their strength. They become noise instead of authority.

Understanding the claimant also means recognising that many claimants assume the living will not question them. This assumption gives them confidence. When they encounter a living being who stands calmly and asks for clarity, their confidence changes. They begin to realise that their routine does not apply. They realise they must rely on truth rather than habit. This realisation often exposes the lack of foundation in their actions.

Understanding the claimant removes the mystique of authority. Authority appears powerful from a distance. Once examined, it becomes clear that most authority is borrowed, not genuine. It is borrowed from belief. It is borrowed from habit. It is borrowed from silence. When the living asks for proof, the borrowed authority must reveal its source. Many cannot. They collapse under examination. This collapse shows the truth behind the system.

Understanding the claimant is essential because it restores balance. The artificial world attempts to position itself above the living. But nothing stands above the living. Systems were created by people. Processes were created by people. Roles were created by people. Authority is given, not taken. When the living understands the claimant, the illusion of hierarchy dissolves. The living stands in truth. Truth places all living beings on equal footing.

A claim has meaning only when the claimant stands behind it openly. A claim has weight only when the claimant can prove it. A claim has influence only when the claimant can answer questions. A claim has authority only when the claimant can demonstrate its origin.

The living does not engage with anonymous claims.

The living does not accept claims without identity.

The living does not obey claims that cannot be supported.

Understanding the claimant means understanding the truth of the claim.

Understanding the truth of the claim means requiring proof.

Requiring proof means the living remains free.

Proof and Identity

Identity is the place where most assumptions begin. The artificial world depends on people accepting an identity that was created for them. This identity is the recorded name. It is the label used by institutions. It is the reference used in documents. It is the foundation of every automated process. People become conditioned to respond whenever this name appears. They act as though the name and the living being are the same. This confusion allows assumptions to grow. Assumptions become obligation. Obligation becomes claimed authority. Understanding identity ends this chain.

Proof and identity are linked because a claim must be directed at the correct identity to have meaning. A claim aimed at a label is not a claim aimed at the living. A label is not a living being. A label has no breath. A label has no awareness. A label cannot agree. A label cannot contract. A label cannot be bound unless the living steps into it knowingly. This step is voluntary. Many people take it automatically. They respond as the name because they were trained to do so since childhood. The sovereign mind breaks this habit by understanding the separation between the living and the record.

The recorded identity is created by institutions. It is a tool. It is used to organise information. It is not the living. Yet most claims arrive addressed to the recorded identity. The artificial world expects the living to take responsibility for these claims. This expectation is the foundation of false authority. If the living does not question the identity being addressed, the system assumes consent. Consent given through habit is not true consent. It is unintentional involvement. It binds the living only because the living does not recognise the distinction.

Proof becomes essential in this area. The living must ask how the claim connects to them. If the claimant states that the notice is addressed to the name, the living asks whether the name is the living. If the claimant insists the name and the living are the same, the living asks for proof. This question often exposes the weakness in the system. Few claimants can explain the link. They rely on the assumption that names equal beings. This assumption is learned, not true. When the living requests proof, the habit begins to break.

Identity is used as a doorway. Once the living steps through it, the system treats the step as agreement. It treats the step as acceptance. It treats the step as voluntary participation. When the living asks for proof of the link, the doorway becomes visible. A visible doorway cannot trap the living. The living decides whether to step through it. This decision must be conscious. Conscious action is the core of sovereignty.

Understanding proof and identity involves recognising that the artificial world operates through roles. The recorded identity is one of these roles. The living can choose to act in the role. They can choose not to. They can decide when the role is appropriate. They can decide when it is not. Institutions assume the role is permanent. They act as though the living cannot separate from it. This is false. The living exists without the role. The role cannot exist without the living. The one who depends on the other cannot be superior to it.

When the living asks for proof that the claim applies to them, they are not refusing involvement. They are asking for clarity. Clarity is necessary before any decision can be made. If the claimant cannot show how the claim binds the living, the claim does not bind the living. Identity does not create obligation unless the living agrees. Agreement must be proven. It cannot be assumed through the presence of a name on a page.

The artificial world strengthens the recorded identity through repetition. People hear the name every day. They write it. They sign it. They answer to it. They internalise it. Over time the recorded identity becomes part of their self-image. They forget it is a label. They forget it is a representation. They forget it was created by others. They accept it as themselves. This acceptance gives systems a tool for influence. When the living forgets the separation, the recorded identity becomes a mechanism for control.

The sovereign mind remains aware of the distinction. It uses the recorded identity when appropriate, but it does not confuse it with the living. It knows that a claim addressed to the name must still show proof before it can influence the living. Proof must connect the claim to the living being. Without this connection, the claim has no force. Many claimants cannot show this connection. They rely on assumption. Assumption is broken by awareness.

Understanding proof and identity removes the emotional influence created by names. Many people react when they see their name on a document. They feel targeted. They feel pressured. They feel responsible. These emotions come from identification. They come from believing the name equals the self. When the living separates from the recorded identity, the pressure dissolves. A name on a document is no longer a command. It is a label attached to a claim. Claims require proof. Labels do not create obligation.

A claim must show more than a name. It must show the source of authority. It must show the origin of the obligation. It must show the agreement that binds the living. If these cannot be shown, the claim has no substance. The living does not act on unproven claims. The living acts only on truth.

Identity also affects how claimants communicate. When they believe the name binds the living, they become confident. They assume they have control. When the living asks for proof of the connection, the claimant often becomes uncertain. Their certainty depended on the assumption. When the assumption is gone, they must rely on evidence. Evidence is rare. Most claims are built on procedure, not truth. Procedure is not proof. Procedure does not bind the living.

Systems also use identity to create the impression of inevitability. They say your account must be settled. They say your name appears on the record. They say action will continue. These statements only matter if the living accepts the identity as themselves. When the living recognises the difference, the statements lose their force. A process cannot continue without the involvement of the living. A name cannot agree to anything. A name cannot be compelled. A name cannot be punished. Only the living can experience the consequences of an action. Proof must show that the action reaches the living. If proof cannot be shown, the action cannot apply.

Understanding proof and identity also reveals the importance of choosing when to engage. The living may choose to respond as the recorded identity when it serves a purpose. They may choose to respond as the living when clarity is required. They may choose to remain separate when the claim has no foundation. Choice is the key. Systems expect automatic engagement. Awareness breaks this pattern. Automatic involvement is replaced with conscious decision. Conscious decision requires proof. Proof must be asked for.

Identity is often used to create pressure because it is personal. People feel exposed when their name is used. They feel singled out. They believe the system knows them. But the system knows only the recorded identity. It does not know the living. It cannot see the living. It cannot act upon the living without their participation. Identity is a tool for influence, not a tool for truth. Truth requires evidence. Evidence must be shown, not assumed.

Understanding proof and identity means recognising that many claims rely on the living forgetting their own nature. The artificial world wants the living to think like the record. When the living thinks like the record, they act predictably. They act automatically. They act without questioning. This benefits the system. The sovereign mind thinks like the living. It remains aware. It remains present. It remains calm. Calmness allows clarity. Clarity allows questions. Questions reveal truth.

The living is not a label. The living is not a role. The living is not a record. The living does not belong to any system. The living cannot be bound by assumption. The living cannot be bound by procedure. The living cannot be bound by appearance. The living can be bound only by conscious agreement. Agreement must be proven. Proof must come before action. Proof must come before obligation. Proof must come before consent.

Where proof does not connect the claim to the living, the claim has no force. Where proof does not show clear authority, the authority does not stand. Where proof does not show a binding agreement, no agreement exists.

The living acts only on truth.

Truth is shown through evidence.

Identity does not replace evidence.

And the living remains free.

Identity is the point where the artificial world makes its strongest assumptions. This is where most claims begin. This is where most people surrender authority without realising it. Every system needs a fixed point to attach its claims to. That fixed point is the recorded identity. It is the entry door through which demands, notices, warnings, and instructions attempt to reach the living. When the living believes the recorded identity and the living being are the same, the system gains silent control. When the living understands the difference, the system loses its foundation.

The recorded identity is not chosen by the living. It is created by others. It is stored in registers. It is printed on documents. It is used to identify a set of information. It is not the living. It is a representation used for administrative convenience. Over time, people learn to step into this representation automatically. They respond when the name is called. They sign where the name appears. They feel responsible for the name. This is a learned behaviour. Learned behaviours can be unlearned. Awareness is the beginning of that process.

The sovereign mind does not reject the recorded identity. It recognises it as a tool. Tools can be used when needed. They can be set aside when not needed. The problem arises only when the living forgets that it is a tool. When the tool becomes the self, assumption replaces truth. Claims aimed at the recorded identity begin to feel personal. They begin to feel binding. They begin to feel unavoidable. This feeling comes from identification, not from evidence.

Proof becomes the test that separates personal involvement from administrative assumption. When a claim is made, the living asks for proof that it reaches them. If the proof cannot be shown, the claim does not reach them. It remains an administrative statement directed at a label. Labels cannot agree. Labels cannot consent. Labels cannot be held responsible. The living decides whether to step into the label. That decision must be conscious. Conscious decisions require evidence, not assumption.

Systems rely on the living stepping into the recorded identity without thinking. They use familiar language to trigger automatic reactions. They use the name to press emotional buttons. They use reference numbers to appear organised. They use headings and formatting to create pressure. None of these create obligation. Obligation must come from agreement. Agreement must be shown. Agreement must involve the living. A name on a page cannot create agreement on its own.

Understanding proof and identity means recognising that identity is used to bridge the gap between the artificial world and the living. The artificial world cannot reach the living directly. It needs a constructed identity. It needs an administrative role. It needs something that exists within its own structure. The recorded identity serves this purpose. When a claim is aimed at the recorded identity, the artificial world assumes the living will respond. This assumption is the weakness. It is the point where proof must be required.

A claim addressed to the recorded identity must show how the living is involved. It must show the origin of obligation. It must show where consent was given. It must show the agreement that binds the living. If these cannot be shown, the claim has no force. The living does not respond from fear. The living responds from clarity. Clarity demands proof.

Identity also influences how the living feels. People often feel exposed when their name appears in letters. They feel seen. They feel singled out. They interpret this as pressure. But pressure comes from belief, not truth. The artificial world does not see the living. It sees a record. It sees data. It sees a number. It sees a file. When the living separates from the recorded identity, the emotional pressure collapses. A claim directed at a record cannot harm the living unless the living chooses to engage with it.

Understanding proof and identity also reveals that many claimants do not understand the distinction themselves. They treat the recorded identity as the living being. They assume authority because they assume the identity binds the living. When asked to show proof of this connection, they struggle. They attempt to avoid the question. They attempt to shift responsibility. They attempt to direct attention back to the document. These behaviours reveal that the assumption is internal, not factual. Internal assumptions are not evidence. They do not bind the living.

The sovereign mind remains steady during these moments. It does not become frustrated. It does not become emotional. It observes. It asks again. It requires clarity. If the claimant cannot provide proof, the claim falls. It does not matter how confident the claimant sounds. It does not matter how firm the language is. It does not matter how official the document appears. Proof is the only standard. Proof cannot be replaced by style.

The artificial world uses identity to create structure. Structure is necessary for administration. But structure is not authority. Structure is a system of organisation. It organizes information. It organizes procedures. It organizes responsibilities within the artificial world. The living does not belong to that structure. The living can interact with it when necessary. But interaction does not create subordination. Interaction does not create obligation. Obligation must be proven. Proof must show that the living agreed to be bound.

Identity also plays a central role in implied consent. Many systems treat behaviour as agreement. When the living responds to letters, they treat it as consent. When the living answers questions, they treat it as consent. When the living steps into the recorded identity without clarity, they treat it as consent. This is how implied contracts are created. Implied contracts rely on habit. Habit relies on identification. When the living becomes aware of their identity, implied consent collapses. The claimant must show explicit agreement. Explicit agreement requires proof.

The sovereign mind knows that identity must be treated with intention. It decides how and when to use the recorded identity. It does not act automatically. It does not step into the role without questioning it. It understands that the recorded identity cannot be the foundation of obligation. The foundation must come from truth. Truth is supported by evidence. Evidence must be shown clearly. Where evidence is absent, the living remains separate.

Understanding proof and identity also prevents confusion. Confusion is used to control. Many claimants speak as though the recorded identity is inseparable from the living. They use language that merges the two. They rely on this merging to strengthen their claim. When the living rejects this merging, the claim weakens. The claimant must show how the two are connected. This is the central weakness of the artificial world. It cannot show this connection. The connection exists only as an assumption. Assumption cannot bind the living.

Identity is also used to create the illusion of inevitability. When a claim is directed at the recorded identity, the system behaves as though the process has already begun. It sends reminders. It sends warnings. It sends escalations. Each new piece of paper suggests progress. But progress cannot occur without participation. A label cannot take action. A label cannot respond. A label cannot generate consequences. Only the living can take action. Proof must show that the living is bound. Without this proof, the process is empty.

The sovereign mind sees this clearly. It does not become concerned with the sequence of documents. It does not assume the recorded identity reflects the living. It remains grounded. It asks for proof. If proof is absent, the sequence has no meaning. The artificial world creates process to appear strong. Strength must come from truth. Truth must be proven.

Understanding proof and identity also empowers the living to remain calm. Calmness is a sign of strength. Calmness shows awareness. Calmness breaks emotional pressure. When identity is understood, emotional triggers disappear. The name on the letter no longer feels like an attack. It feels like a label. Labels are harmless unless the living gives them meaning. Meaning must be chosen. The sovereign mind chooses truth, not fear.

Identity is a tool. It is not the living. When the living remembers this, the artificial world loses its grip. Claims that once felt heavy begin to look empty. Notices that once created fear become ordinary. Letters that once demanded action become simple statements. Statements must be supported. Support must come from evidence. Evidence must be shown by the claimant.

Where proof is absent, identity cannot bind.

Where identity cannot bind, authority cannot stand.

Where authority cannot stand, the living remains free.

Proof exposes the separation.

Identity reveals the structure.

Awareness protects the living.

The living accepts nothing without clarity.

The living accepts nothing without truth.

The living accepts nothing without proof.

When a Claim Lacks Evidence

A claim without evidence is not a claim. It is noise. It is an attempt to create influence through words alone. When a claim lacks evidence, it reveals its own weakness. It relies on tone, presentation, or pressure to appear strong. It hopes the living will act before thinking. It hopes the living will obey out of habit. It hopes the living will fear consequences that have not been proven. These hopes are the foundation of false authority. When the living requires evidence, these hopes collapse.

The artificial world produces claims constantly. Notices, letters, warnings, demands, reminders, statements. Each one appears serious. Each one implies responsibility. Each one suggests that action must be taken. But implication is not evidence. Suggestion is not truth. Words printed on a page do not create authority. Authority must be shown through proof. Without proof, the claim cannot stand.

Many claims lack evidence because the claimant expects no one to ask for it. They rely on silence. Silence is their strongest tool. Silence allows the claim to appear real. Silence allows fear to grow. Silence allows assumption to shape behaviour. When the living breaks silence, the claim must be supported. A claim unsupported is a claim exposed. Exposure dissolves authority.

Understanding what a claim without evidence looks like is essential to sovereignty. Many claims present as complete statements but fall apart when examined. The sovereign mind examines them calmly, without fear. It asks simple questions. It seeks clarity. It requires truth. Evidence must appear. If it does not, the claim falls away.

A claim lacking evidence often relies on repeated phrases instead of substance. It uses terms such as mandatory, required, urgent, outstanding, owed. These terms are used to provoke emotion rather than to present truth. They are designed to create urgency. Urgency removes thought. Thought removes illusion. When the living reads carefully, the emotional force of these words weakens. They become hollow without proof to support them.

A claim lacking evidence also uses vague references. It may mention rules, procedures, processes, or obligations. But none of these are identified clearly. They are used as weight, not as fact. The living asks, what rule. The living asks, what process. The living asks, what obligation. If the claimant cannot show the exact foundation, the concept is meaningless. Vague references are not evidence. They are distractions.

A claim lacking evidence often shifts responsibility. Instead of proving the claim, the claimant demands information. They demand explanation. They demand action. This reversal is a tactic. It places pressure on the living. It creates the illusion that the living must justify themselves. The sovereign mind does not fall for this. The living asks the claimant to justify their own words. Words require proof. The one who makes the claim must support it.

A claim lacking evidence becomes visible through inconsistency. When asked for clarity, the claimant may provide answers that contradict earlier statements. Contradictions reveal the absence of truth. Truth is simple. It does not conflict with itself. False authority struggles to maintain consistency. Each question reveals new weaknesses.

A claim lacking evidence may also rely on escalation. The claimant threatens further action. They suggest that consequences will increase. They imply urgency. This escalation is used to create fear. But fear does not create proof. Fear does not create authority. Fear does not create obligation. The living recognises escalation as a sign of weakness. When a claim is strong, it does not rely on threats. It rests on evidence.

A claim lacking evidence reveals itself when the claimant becomes uncomfortable with questions. A confident claimant answers directly. A claimant standing in truth does not avoid clarity. A claimant relying on procedure will struggle. They will become defensive. They will take offence. They will repeat their demand without explaining its basis. These reactions are signs that evidence is missing.

The sovereign mind watches these signs calmly. It understands that the claimant's reactions reveal the truth of the situation. When the claimant avoids the question, the claim is weak. When the claimant becomes aggressive, the claim is unsupported. When the claimant attempts to intimidate, the claim lacks foundation. These observations allow the living to remain steady. Steadiness is strength.

A claim lacking evidence often hides behind formality. Formality creates an atmosphere of authority. It uses structured formatting. It uses references. It uses institutional language. This creates the illusion of legitimacy. But formality is not proof. Formality is appearance. Appearance cannot bind the living. Only truth can. The living sees past the presentation. The living looks for substance. Substance must be shown. If substance is missing, the claim is without merit.

A claim lacking evidence often tries to rely on the recorded identity to create obligation. It assumes that addressing the recorded identity automatically binds the living. This is false. The living requires proof of connection. If the claimant cannot show the agreement that binds the living, the use of the name is irrelevant. A name cannot be bound. A name cannot be compelled. A name cannot consent. The living remains separate until evidence connects them.

A claim lacking evidence may also hide behind collective behaviour. Many people accept similar claims. Many people comply without question. This creates the illusion of consensus. Consensus is not evidence. Consensus is habit. Habit cannot replace truth. A claim is not validated by the number of people who obey it. It is validated only by the evidence supporting it. The living does not follow crowds. The living follows truth.

A claim lacking evidence is often built on assumption rather than foundation. It assumes authority. It assumes obligation. It assumes consent. The sovereign mind recognises assumption instantly. Assumption cannot stand when asked to prove itself. Proof is the antidote to assumption. Proof reveals reality. When assumption and reality clash, reality remains.

A claim lacking evidence also shows itself through urgency. Urgent claims attempt to bypass thought. They demand quick action. Quick action prevents examination. Examination reveals the lack of evidence. When the living slows the interaction, the urgency loses force. If a claim cannot survive time, it cannot survive scrutiny. Truth remains steady regardless of time. False authority demands speed because it cannot stand still.

A claim lacking evidence may try to wrap itself in complexity. It may use technical language. It may reference codes. It may quote processes. Complexity creates confusion. Confusion prevents clarity. Clarity demands simplicity. The sovereign mind does not get lost in technical language. It returns to the simple question, what is the proof. Without proof, complexity is irrelevant. Without proof, technical language becomes noise.

A claim lacking evidence is often exposed by the claimant's inability to show origin. Origin is the foundation of authority. Authority must come from truth. Truth must come from a clear source. A claimant must know the origin of their power. If the claimant cannot identify the origin, the power does not exist. Many claimants operate without understanding their own limits. They act from routine, not truth. The living requires truth, not routine.

A claim lacking evidence may rely on repetition. The same statements appear in multiple notices. The same phrases are used. The same warnings are repeated. Repetition is used to create a sense of inevitability. But repeating a claim does not make it true. Repetition does not create proof. The living sees repetition as a sign of automation. Automation is not authority. Automation cannot stand when the living asks for proof.

A claim lacking evidence becomes powerless when the living remains calm. Calmness is the foundation of awareness. Awareness dissolves fear. Fear is the tool used to maintain the illusion of legitimacy. The living separates emotion from truth. Truth requires evidence, not emotion. When emotion fades, the claim loses its strongest weapon.

A claim lacking evidence has only one weakness. It cannot show what it claims. This weakness is exposed with a single question. A simple request for proof reveals everything. The claimant must either provide evidence or avoid the question. Avoidance is the answer. Avoidance shows the claim has no foundation.

The sovereign mind requires proof because proof protects the living. Proof prevents assumption from becoming authority. Proof prevents habit from becoming obligation. Proof prevents fear from becoming decision. Proof restores balance. Balance restores clarity. Clarity restores sovereignty.

Where evidence is absent, there is no claim.

Where proof is missing, there is no authority.

Where truth cannot be shown, the living remains free.

Evidence is the line that separates reality from assumption. Without evidence, a claim has no standing. It has no substance. It has no truth behind it. It is nothing more than an attempt to influence behaviour. Yet most claims in the artificial world carry no evidence. They carry expectations, not truth. They carry pressure, not proof. They carry formatting, not foundation. When the living understands this, the interaction changes entirely. What once felt powerful becomes ordinary. What once felt inevitable becomes optional. What once felt dangerous becomes irrelevant.

A claim without evidence exposes itself through its behaviour. It cannot stand still. It always tries to move the living. It pushes. It pressures. It attempts to provoke a response. This is because a claim with no evidence cannot support itself. It must lean on the reaction of the living. If the living does not react, the claim falls. This is why systems send repeated notices. This is why they escalate language. This is why they shorten timelines. All of these behaviours are attempts to push the living forward before the claim collapses under its own emptiness.

The sovereign mind remains still. Stillness is power. Stillness forces the claim to stand on its own. If it cannot, it dissolves. When the living asks for proof, they require the claimant to stand without leaning on fear or urgency. Most claimants cannot do this. They expect the living to carry the weight of the interaction. They expect the living to assume the burden. They expect the living to accept responsibility that was never proven. When the living refuses, the weakness becomes visible.

A claim without evidence often displays confusion when questioned. The claimant may provide circular answers. They may repeat the same phrases. They may direct the living back to the document. They may use broad statements rather than specifics. Circular answers show that there is no foundation. Repetition shows that there is no substance. Redirecting attention shows avoidance. Broad statements hide lack of detail. Each of these signals reveals that the claim cannot survive scrutiny.

The sovereign mind does not accept confusion as an answer. Confusion is a tactic. It is used to overwhelm thought. When the living slows down and listens carefully, the tactic loses force. The living remains calm. Calmness reveals that the claimant is struggling. A struggling claimant exposes the truth that the claim lacks evidence.

Another sign of a claim without evidence is inconsistency. When pressed, the claimant may change the basis of the claim. They may introduce new terms. They may contradict their earlier statements. They may retreat from certainty. Inconsistency is the enemy of truth. Truth is simple. Truth is steady. Truth does not change under pressure. Only false authority shifts when questioned. When the foundation of a claim changes, it exposes that the foundation never existed.

The sovereign mind uses questions to reveal these shifts. A single question can expose inconsistency. A calm question creates clarity. When a claimant answers one way today and another way tomorrow, the living sees the weakness. The claim cannot stand. The claimant is adjusting their position to maintain control. Control maintained through adjustment is not truth. It is manipulation. Manipulation cannot bind the living.

A claim without evidence often hides behind policy. Policy is used as a replacement for authority. The claimant says it is policy. They believe this settles the matter. It does not. Policy is an internal rule. It applies to the organisation, not the living. Policy cannot bind the living being. Only agreements can bind the living. Policy cannot replace evidence. When the living asks for proof of agreement, policy becomes irrelevant. Policy cannot answer this question. It stands exposed as an internal tool, not a source of authority.

The sovereign mind does not argue about policy. It questions the basis of authority. Authority must be shown. Authority must be proven. Authority must exist independent of organisational preference. When the living asks for the origin of authority, policy is revealed as a distraction. The claimant must move beyond it. If they cannot, the claim has no foundation.

A claim without evidence also uses incomplete information. It presents part of a picture and hopes the living will assume the rest. This is intentional. Incomplete information creates space for fear. The mind fills gaps with imagined consequences. These imagined consequences pressure the living into action. But action based on imagination is not sovereignty. It is surrender. The living must see the whole picture. Proof shows the whole picture. Without proof, the picture is fiction.

The sovereign mind does not fill gaps with imagination. It fills them with questions. Each question removes uncertainty. Each answer provides clarity. When the claimant cannot answer fully, the incompleteness remains. The incompleteness becomes the evidence that the claim is false. A claim must be whole. If it is not whole, it is not truth.

A claim without evidence often uses the recorded identity as its anchor. It relies on the living reacting to the presence of their name. It assumes responsibility where none has been proven. It assumes connection where none has been shown. The artificial world treats the recorded identity as the gateway. But a gateway must be opened consciously. If the living does not open the gate, the claim cannot reach them. If the living asks for proof of the connection, the claimant must demonstrate how the living is involved.

Most claimants cannot. They assume the question will never be asked. They assume the recorded identity automatically binds the living. This assumption is their weakness. When the living requires evidence of the connection, the claim loses force. The claimant must prove that the living agreed to be bound by the recorded identity. That agreement must be shown. It cannot be assumed. Where it cannot be shown, the claim has no foundation.

A claim without evidence becomes exposed when the claimant relies on threats. Threats are used when truth is missing. A strong claim does not need threats. It stands calmly. It stands on fact. It stands on authority that can be proven. Threats reveal insecurity. They reveal weakness. They show that the claimant is attempting to control the living through fear rather than through truth.

The sovereign mind sees threats as signals. They do not create fear. They reveal the absence of evidence. The living does not react to threats. It responds to truth. Truth must be shown. If truth is absent, threats lose meaning.

A claim without evidence often attempts to shame the living. It suggests responsibility. It implies wrongdoing. It uses guilt as a tool. But guilt without proof is manipulation. Manipulation is not authority. Manipulation cannot bind the living. Guilt exists only when the living accepts it. The living does not accept guilt without evidence. Evidence must show wrongdoing. If evidence is missing, the suggestion is meaningless.

The sovereign mind stays grounded. It does not internalise pressure. It does not internalise judgement. It does not internalise guilt. It asks for proof. Proof must be objective. Proof must be clear. Proof must be shown. Without it, the claim dissolves.

A claim without evidence reveals itself through the claimant's discomfort. When questioned, they shift their tone. They become uncertain. They attempt to regain control. These behaviours show that the claim has no solid base. A solid claim remains steady. A weak claim shakes.

The living observes the shaking. The shaking reveals the truth. The living remains calm. Calmness is the mirror that shows the claimant their own instability. Instability is weakness. Weakness cannot bind the living.

A claim without evidence may also disappear when pressed. Many claimants simply stop responding when asked for proof. They retreat. They withdraw. They cease communication. This silence reveals everything. A claim supported by truth does not disappear. It continues. A claim supported by assumption retreats when questioned. Retreat is admission. It shows that the claim cannot stand.

The sovereign mind recognises that retreat is resolution. A claim that cannot survive questions has answered itself. The answer is no authority. The answer is no obligation. The answer is no binding force.

Evidence is the only measure of truth.

Without evidence, there is no truth.

Without truth, there is no authority.

Without authority, the living remains free.

A claim without evidence collapses when touched. It needed fear to survive. Fear disappears under awareness. Awareness comes from calmness. Calmness comes from the living knowing their own authority.

The living requires evidence because evidence protects them. Evidence reveals whether the claim is real or imagined. Evidence separates truth from pressure. Evidence is the foundation of sovereignty.

Where evidence is absent, sovereignty remains untouched.

Proof Protects the Living

Proof is protection. It shields the living from manipulation. It prevents false authority from gaining ground. It removes fear. It restores clarity. It prevents the artificial world from shaping behaviour through assumption, pressure, or routine. Proof creates a barrier between the living and anything that lacks truth. This barrier is not aggressive. It does not attack. It does not challenge for the sake of conflict. It stands quietly. It stands firmly. It stands without fear. Truth needs no force. It needs only evidence.

The living is safest when standing on truth. Truth does not shift. Truth does not bend. Truth does not retreat. When the living stands on truth, false authority cannot reach them. Claims collapse. Threats lose their effect. Assumptions become visible. Illusions fall apart. Proof exposes the real from the imagined. The artificial world thrives on imagination. It does not thrive on scrutiny. Scrutiny demands proof. Proof clears away illusions.

Many people underestimate the power of proof. They believe they need complex knowledge to protect themselves. They believe they need legal language. They believe they need specialised understanding. They do not. Protection comes from simple questions. Questions lead to proof. Proof leads to truth. Truth reveals whether the claim has substance. Most claims do not. Once the living sees this clearly, their fear evaporates.

Proof protects the living because it removes confusion. Confusion is one of the strongest tools used against people. Confusion creates hesitation. Confusion creates uncertainty. Uncertainty invites fear. Fear invites compliance. Compliance appears to validate false authority. Proof cuts through confusion. It forces clarity. Clarity removes fear. Fear cannot survive in the presence of truth.

Proof protects the living by slowing the interaction. Pressure demands speed. Proof demands time. When the living asks for evidence, everything stops. The claimant cannot push forward until the evidence is shown. Many claimants do not expect this. They expect the living to act quickly. They expect automatic responses. They expect compliance. Proof interrupts this expectation. It requires the claimant to justify their words before action takes place.

This change in pace shifts control back to the living. The living no longer reacts. The living reflects. Reflection leads to understanding. Understanding leads to confidence. Confidence removes fear. This is how proof protects the living not by confrontation, but by restoring balance.

Proof protects the living because it forces the claimant to reveal their limits. Most claimants do not understand their own limits. They act within procedures. They follow scripts. They rely on institutional practices. When asked for proof, they must step outside the script. They must show something real. Many cannot. When they cannot, their authority collapses. A claimant who cannot explain their authority has no authority. Proof makes this visible.

Proof also protects the living by revealing hidden assumptions. Many claims are built on invisible expectations. These expectations are never stated openly. They hide behind tone. They hide behind formatting. They hide behind tradition. They hide behind the recorded identity. When the living asks for proof, the assumptions surface. False authority cannot survive in the open. Once assumptions are visible, they lose influence. Proof brings them into the light.

Proof protects the living by preventing unintended agreements. Agreements can be created through behaviour. Silence can be mistaken for consent. Quick responses can be mistaken for acceptance. Even fear-based compliance can be interpreted as agreement. Proof breaks this pattern. When the living requires evidence before acting, they create space for clarity. Agreements cannot form in that space unless the living chooses them. Proof protects the living by ensuring that no contract forms without conscious intention.

Proof protects the living because it exposes automation. Automated processes cannot answer questions. They cannot provide evidence. They cannot explain the origin of authority. They cannot show how the claim reaches the living. When the living asks for proof, the system must switch from automation to a human response. A human claimant must step forward. Automation cannot hide behind procedure when proof is required. Automation loses power. The living remains protected.

Proof also protects the living by revealing inconsistencies. False claims are unstable. They shift. They contradict themselves. They change shape when questioned. Truth does not. When the living requests proof, the inconsistency becomes visible. The claimant stumbles. They adjust their story. They alter the foundation of the claim. These shifts reveal the lack of truth. Proof exposes the instability.

The sovereign mind does not become emotional when inconsistencies appear. It observes. It remains calm. It sees the weakness. The weakness protects the living. A claim built on shifting ground cannot stand against awareness.

Proof protects the living by removing personalisation. Many people feel personally attacked when they receive a claim. They think the demand is directed at them. They internalise it. They react emotionally. Proof removes this reaction. It reframes the interaction. A claim is no longer a personal attack. It is simply a statement made by someone that requires evidence. Once depersonalised, the emotional charge disappears. Protection follows naturally.

Proof protects the living by demanding honesty. Dishonest claims rely on fear, confusion, and pressure. When the living requires proof, dishonesty becomes risky. The claimant must either lie openly or reveal their weakness. Lying openly exposes the claimant. Revealing weakness dissolves authority. Either outcome protects the living. Truth survives scrutiny. Lies do not.

Proof protects the living by clarifying the relationship. The artificial world treats the living as subordinate. It behaves as though the living has no right to question. It behaves as though authority must be obeyed. When the living asks for proof, the relationship changes. The living places themselves on equal ground with the claimant. Equal ground is essential. Equal ground removes the illusion of hierarchy. The living cannot be controlled by someone who cannot prove their authority.

Proof protects the living by restoring awareness of identity. When a claim is directed at the recorded identity, proof forces the claimant to explain the connection. If the claimant cannot show how the living is bound by the recorded identity, the bond dissolves. This protects the living from false obligations. Identity without proof cannot bind. Proof protects the living from being pulled into the role unknowingly.

Proof protects the living by removing fear of consequences. Consequences gain power only when the claim appears valid. Once the living asks for proof, the fear loses force. If the claimant cannot show the consequences are real, they disappear. Fear fades. The living regains control. Proof protects the living by dissolving imagined danger.

Proof protects the living by making the claimant responsible for their claims. Responsibility is important. Without responsibility, anyone can make demands. Anyone can impose expectations. Anyone can attempt to control another. Proof forces accountability. A claimant who makes a claim must stand behind it. They must show its origin. They must show its truth. They must show its authority. If they cannot, the claim falls.

Proof protects the living because it forces every part of the interaction into the open. False authority hides. True authority stands in the light. Proof shines the light. It is the lens through which the living sees the truth. Without proof, the artificial world would rely entirely on illusion. With proof, illusion cannot survive.

Proof protects the living by empowering them. Power does not come from force. It comes from awareness. When the living knows they have the right to require proof, they stand differently. They speak differently. They think differently. They no longer act out of fear. They no longer follow blindly. They no longer surrender authority. They remain calm, steady, and present. Presence is power. Awareness is protection. Proof is the foundation that makes awareness possible.

Where proof is required, false authority cannot stand.

Where proof is demanded, illusion dissolves.

Where proof is the standard, the living remains safe.

Proof protects the living because truth protects the living.

Truth protects because truth cannot be shaped by fear.

Truth stands.

And the living stands with it.

Proof is the shield the living carries into every interaction. It does not look like a shield. It does not feel like a shield. It is not made of force. It is not made of opposition. It is made of clarity. Clarity protects better than resistance ever could. Resistance invites conflict. Clarity dissolves it. Resistance creates friction. Clarity removes it. Proof is not about force. Proof is about truth. And truth is the strongest protection the living can stand upon.

False authority thrives when people forget to ask for proof. It survives when people react emotionally. It survives when people assume the claim must be valid. It survives when people answer without thinking. These conditions keep the living vulnerable. Proof reverses all of them. Proof restores thought. Proof demands understanding. Proof brings the living into awareness. Awareness is the natural defence against manipulation.

Proof protects the living from confusion by turning vague claims into clear ones. When a claimant makes a broad statement, the living does not accept it. The living asks for the details. Details expose the truth. Many claims cannot withstand detail. They collapse under explanation because they were never built on evidence. Proof forces each claim to become specific. Specificity is where false authority fails.

Proof protects the living from intimidation. Intimidation depends on emotion, not truth. A claimant may use strong language. They may use strict tone. They may use bold formatting. These tools aim to provoke fear. Fear blocks thought. Fear triggers compliance. But fear cannot stand where proof is required. Proof removes emotion. It directs attention away from tone and onto substance. When attention returns to substance, intimidation fades.

Proof protects the living from urgency. Urgency is used to prevent questioning. It forces people to act quickly. Acting quickly prevents reflection. Reflection exposes weakness. Weakness destroys false authority. When the living asks for proof, urgency loses meaning. The claimant must pause. They must answer. They must provide evidence. Many cannot. When they cannot, the urgency evaporates. It becomes clear that the pressure had no foundation.

Proof protects the living by revealing the boundaries of authority. Most claimants do not understand their own limits. They assume authority because others obey them. They imagine authority because their role suggests it. They expect authority because people rarely challenge them. Proof demands that authority be shown, not assumed. A claimant who cannot explain the scope of their authority reveals its absence. Once the absence is visible, the living is protected. They no longer feel pressure to obey what cannot be proven.

Proof protects the living by stopping manipulation in its earliest form. Manipulation begins with suggestion. Suggestion becomes assumption. Assumption becomes behaviour. Behaviour becomes expectation. Expectation becomes obligation. Proof stops this cycle at the first step. A suggestion cannot become assumption if the living asks for proof. A suggestion must be supported. If it cannot be supported, it returns to being nothing more than a suggestion.

Proof protects the living by preventing automatic agreement. Automatic agreement is the greatest weakness a person can have in the artificial world. It is the source of almost all silent contracts. It is how systems gain influence without permission. Automatic agreement happens when the living acts without thinking. Proof forces thinking. Thinking prevents automatic action. When thought returns, agreement requires intention. Intentional agreement protects the living. Unintentional agreement binds them. Proof separates the two.

Proof protects the living from emotional triggers. Many claimants rely on emotional tactics. They use blame. They use shame. They use guilt. They use urgency. They use repetition. These tactics are used because they work on people who do not understand their own authority. But proof does not operate on emotion. It operates on evidence. When the living focuses on evidence, emotion fades. Emotional tactics lose their power. The living becomes steady.

Proof protects the living from illusion. The artificial world creates illusions of authority. It uses symbols to create the appearance of power. It uses formatting to create the appearance of legitimacy. It uses official language to create the appearance of truth. These illusions work only when unexamined. Proof forces examination. Examination reveals that symbols are not authority. Formatting is not truth. Language is not evidence. The illusion falls apart under scrutiny. Once the illusion breaks, influence disappears.

Proof protects the living from unwanted contracts. Contracts require agreement. Agreement requires clarity. Clarity requires proof. Without proof, no contract can be considered valid. But the artificial world tries to form contracts through behaviour. It treats silence as acceptance. It treats compliance as intention. It treats fear as agreement. Proof disrupts this. When the living asks for proof before acting, no unwanted agreement can form. The living chooses when and how they bind themselves. Nothing binds them without their awareness.

Proof protects the living from hidden assumptions about identity. When a claim is directed at the recorded identity, the claimant expects the living to step into that identity without question. They expect the living to take responsibility for the label. But labels are not the living. The living requires proof of the connection. When that proof cannot be shown, the claim loses its ability to reach the living. Identity becomes a boundary. Proof protects that boundary.

Proof protects the living from procedures that lack truth. Many claimants rely on procedure rather than evidence. They say this is how it is done. They say this is the process. They say this is the correct path. Procedures do not create authority. Procedures are internal tools. They guide organisations, not the living. When the living asks for the lawful basis, procedure collapses. It cannot stand alone. The living remains protected by requiring the truth behind the procedure.

Proof protects the living by exposing inconsistencies. False authority cannot maintain a stable story. It shifts. It contradicts itself. It relies on vague statements that change when pressed. Truth is steady. It does not shift with pressure. When the living asks for proof, inconsistencies become visible. Visibility protects the living. It shows where the claim breaks. A broken claim cannot bind the living.

Proof protects the living by placing responsibility where it belongs. The claimant must support their claim. They must explain themselves. They must show evidence. They must stand behind their words. False authority tries to shift responsibility to the living. It demands explanations. It demands compliance. It demands participation without justification. Proof reverses this. The claimant becomes responsible. The living remains protected.

Proof protects the living from escalation that has no foundation. Many claimants escalate their language because they cannot provide proof. They hope the living will submit under pressure. They increase the severity of their statements. They shorten deadlines. They present imaginary consequences. Consequences are real only when supported by lawful authority. Proof exposes whether authority exists. Where authority is absent, escalation is meaningless.

Proof protects the living by giving them time. Time is essential. False authority moves quickly. It wants to overwhelm. It wants to prevent questions. It wants to rush the living into fear. Proof slows everything. It demands answers. Answers take time. Time exposes weakness. Time reveals truth. Time brings clarity. Clarity protects the living.

Proof protects the living by preventing confusion between confidence and authority. Many claimants speak with confidence. Confidence is not truth. Confidence is a tone. Confidence can be used to mask weakness. When the living asks for proof, tone becomes irrelevant. Authority must be demonstrated. A claimant who cannot demonstrate authority stands exposed. This exposure protects the living.

Proof protects the living because it is simple. Simplicity removes confusion. Simplicity removes noise. Simplicity cuts through intimidation. All the living needs to ask is, what is the proof. This question opens the conversation. It reveals everything. If the claimant has evidence, they will present it calmly. If they do not, they will avoid the question. Avoidance is the answer. Avoidance shows the claim has no foundation.

Proof protects the living by strengthening awareness. Awareness is the core of sovereignty. Awareness prevents manipulation. Awareness prevents fear. Awareness prevents confusion. Awareness protects the living because it brings truth forward. Proof is the tool that reveals truth.

The living stands on proof because proof stands on truth.

Truth protects the living because truth cannot be shaped by fear.

Truth does not rush.

Truth does not panic.

Truth does not threaten.

Truth stands.

And the living stands with truth.

Standing in Calm Authority

Calm authority is the natural state of the living when they stand in truth. It does not require aggression. It does not require defiance. It does not require confrontation. Calm authority is not loud. It is not forceful. It is not dramatic. It is steady. It is clear. It is present. The artificial world expects resistance or compliance. It is prepared for both. It is not prepared for calm authority. Calm authority disables false power because it removes every tool the artificial world depends on.

Calm authority begins with awareness. Awareness means the living understands their own position. They understand the difference between the living and the recorded identity. They understand the difference between a claim and truth. They understand that authority must be proven. They understand that pressure cannot replace evidence. Awareness removes fear because fear is born from confusion. When confusion is gone, fear has nothing to hold onto.

Calm authority is powerful because it cannot be manipulated. Manipulation depends on emotion. It depends on reaction. It depends on urgency. It depends on assumptions. When the living remains calm, these tools lose their effect. A calm disposition makes the claimant reveal themselves. It forces them to rely on truth instead of on pressure. If truth is missing, the claimant becomes exposed. Calmness pulls the mask away.

Standing in calm authority does not mean refusing everything. It means requiring truth in everything. The living listens. The living considers. The living asks for clarity. The living seeks understanding. The living chooses based on truth, not on fear. Calm authority is a posture. It is the posture of someone who knows they are not subject to assumption. It is the posture of someone who knows they cannot be bound without consent. It is the posture of someone who knows that proof protects them.

Calm authority is steady because it does not rush. False authority rushes. It demands quick decisions. It presses for immediate action. This is done to prevent questions. A question slows everything. A slow pace is dangerous for false authority. Calm authority creates pace. It maintains a rhythm based on truth. The living speaks slowly. The living thinks slowly. The living reads slowly. This slow pace dissolves pressure. Pressure needs speed. Calmness robs it of its force.

Calm authority is not defensive. The living does not explain themselves to false authority. The living does not justify themselves. Justification is demanded only by claimants who lack proof. When the living is calm, they do not fall into this trap. They respond with simple questions. They request clarity. They remain grounded. Grounded people cannot be pushed. They cannot be intimidated. They cannot be led into emotional reactions.

Calm authority comes from understanding that the living has no obligation to respond to unproven claims. Many people feel forced to answer every notice. They feel pressured to explain themselves. They feel they must defend their actions. Calm authority removes this belief. The living knows that only claims supported by evidence require engagement. Everything else is noise. Noise cannot bind the living. It can only influence them if they allow it.

Calm authority also comes from recognising that the claimant often relies on a perceived hierarchy. They expect the living to feel lower. They expect the living to feel subordinate. They expect the living to obey the title, the tone, or the formatting. Calm authority removes the hierarchy. It recognises that all living beings stand equal. No one stands above the living without proof. No one has automatic authority over the living. Authority must be earned through truth. Without truth, authority is nothing more than performance.

The sovereign mind does not participate in performance. Performance cannot control someone who is aware. Many claimants act as though their role carries unquestionable legitimacy. When calm authority stands before them, their tone changes. Their confidence weakens. Their assumptions become visible. They realise the living is not distracted by appearance. This shift forces them into honesty, because performance no longer works.

Calm authority protects the living by keeping the interaction simple. Simplicity removes confusion. The living asks one question at a time. They seek one point of clarity at a time. They do not allow the claimant to complicate the situation. False authority thrives in complexity. Complexity creates distraction. Distraction prevents understanding. Calm authority refuses complexity. It demands clear, simple answers. It demands evidence. It demands truth.

Calm authority listens carefully. Listening is a powerful skill. Many people do not listen. They react. They interrupt. They argue. These behaviours make them easy to influence. They reveal insecurity. False authority knows how to exploit insecurity. Calm authority listens without reacting. It observes tone. It observes behaviour. It observes avoidance. It observes inconsistency. These observations provide clarity. Clarity provides protection.

Calm authority uses silence as a tool. Silence unsettles false authority. False authority expects noise. It expects argument. It expects fear. It expects submission. Silence interrupts these expectations. Silence creates space. Space forces the claimant to fill it with something real or to reveal the absence of truth. Many claimants struggle with silence. They attempt to regain control by speaking more aggressively. This aggression exposes their weakness. Calm authority remains steady.

Calm authority does not become overwhelmed. Overwhelm is the result of trying to respond to everything at once. The sovereign mind responds to one point at a time. One claim. One question. One request for proof. This approach prevents overwhelm. It keeps the interaction grounded. It protects the living from confusion.

Calm authority recognises that not every claim deserves a response. Many claims are automated. Many are baseless. Many are attempts to provoke. Calm authority ignores what lacks merit. Ignoring a baseless claim is not avoidance. It is awareness. It is the recognition that only truth deserves attention. Attention is valuable. The living must choose where to place it. Proof decides where attention goes.

Calm authority remains centred. Centred means the living is not pulled by fear or anger. These emotions are used to create instability. Instability leads to mistakes. False authority depends on mistakes. When the living remains centred, mistakes disappear. The interaction becomes simple. Clear. Steady. Authority collapses when the living is centred because it cannot hook into anything. There is no emotion to exploit. There is no panic. There is no confusion. There is only truth.

Calm authority is grounded in the understanding that the living is not required to endure aggression. If a claimant becomes aggressive, the living does not respond in kind. They remain calm. Calmness reveals the aggression for what it is a sign of weakness. Aggression is never a sign of true authority. It is a sign that authority is missing. The claimant uses force because they lack truth. Truth does not require force. It stands quietly.

Calm authority becomes a mirror. It reflects the claimant's behaviour back to them. If the claimant is calm, the interaction remains steady. If the claimant becomes evasive, the evasion becomes visible. If the claimant becomes aggressive, the aggression exposes the weakness of the claim. Calm authority does not need to expose the claimant. The claimant exposes themselves simply by responding to steadiness.

Calm authority is not achieved through defiance. Defiance is emotional. False authority can manipulate defiance. It can claim the living is being difficult. It can paint the living as unreasonable. Calm authority cannot be manipulated. It is clear. It is simple. It is grounded. A calm person asking for proof cannot be criticised without exposing the critic. The system does not know how to deal with calm people asking simple questions.

Calm authority protects the living by creating space for truth. Truth needs space. It needs silence. It needs clarity. False authority thrives only in noise. Noise distracts. Noise confuses. Noise overwhelms. When the living remains calm, the noise cannot take hold. The noise fades. What remains is the truth of the interaction. When truth appears, false authority disappears.

Calm authority is steady because it is rooted in the knowledge that nothing can bind the living without their consent. Consent must be given intentionally. It must be based on truth, not fear. It must be based on evidence, not appearance. The artificial world tries to obtain consent through confusion. Calm authority sees through the confusion. It refuses to act without proof. It refuses to agree without clarity. It refuses to be led by pressure.

Calm authority stands because truth stands.

Truth does not rush.

Truth does not panic.

Truth does not hide.

When the living stands in calm authority, the artificial world loses control.

When the artificial world loses control, truth becomes visible.

When truth becomes visible, sovereignty becomes natural.

The living stands calm.

The living stands aware.

The living stands free.

Calm authority is a state of clarity. It is the point where the living knows what is true and what is not. It is the point where fear no longer shapes decisions. It is the point where the artificial world loses influence. Calm authority does not shout. It does not argue. It does not respond with force. It stands. It observes. It asks. It waits. False authority cannot operate in this space because it depends on confusion, fear, and urgency. Calmness removes all three.

Calm authority protects the living because it keeps the interaction grounded. When the living reacts emotionally, they leave the ground. They enter a space where fear, anger, or anxiety speaks for them. This is where false authority takes control. It knows how to manipulate emotions. It knows how to use tone to provoke. It knows how to use language to unsettle. When the living remains calm, these tools fail. Calmness keeps the mind clear. A clear mind cannot be manipulated.

Calm authority begins with the understanding that the living owes nothing to unproven claims. People often feel pressure to justify themselves. They feel they must explain their actions. They feel they must show compliance. This belief comes from conditioning. Conditioning teaches people that demands must be answered. Calm authority removes this belief. The living knows that only claims supported by truth deserve attention. Everything else is noise.

Calm authority is not passive. It is deliberate. It is controlled. It is intentional. The living chooses their words carefully. They choose their pace. They choose their presence. They do not allow the claimant to dictate the rhythm of the interaction. Rhythm is important. False authority relies on speed. It relies on pushing the living into action before they can think. Calm authority slows everything down. It shifts the pace. This shift disarms manipulation.

Calm authority listens more than it speaks. Listening reveals everything. Listening shows the claimant's tone. It shows their confidence. It shows their uncertainty. It shows their evasions. It shows their contradictions. When the living listens without rushing to respond, the truth surfaces naturally. The claimant exposes themselves through their own words. Calm authority does not have to force this. It happens automatically.

Calm authority does not allow escalation to change the interaction. False authority escalates when it feels weak. It increases the severity of its statements. It shortens timeframes. It amplifies language. It uses forceful words to create fear. But escalation is not proof. Escalation is a sign of weakness. When the living is calm, escalation becomes transparent. It loses its power. It becomes a display rather than a threat.

Calm authority is also rooted in the understanding that silence is powerful. Silence creates space. It forces the claimant to act without guidance. False authority expects reactions. When the living remains silent after a vague statement, the claimant must provide clarity. Many cannot. They reveal their lack of foundation by filling the silence with repetition or avoidance. Silence exposes them. Calm authority uses silence intentionally.

Calm authority rejects emotional traps. False authority often uses guilt to control people. It implies responsibility. It implies wrongdoing. It implies expectation. Guilt is used to make people comply without proof. Calm authority sees guilt as manipulation. The living does not accept guilt that is not proven. Proof is required. If evidence of wrongdoing is absent, guilt is irrelevant. The living remains steady.

Calm authority also rejects shame. Shame is used to create emotional compliance. It makes people feel small. Small people surrender. Calm authority does not become small. It recognises shame as a tactic. It does not internalise it. It does not respond emotionally. It remains grounded. Grounded individuals cannot be shamed into action. They act only on truth.

Calm authority rejects urgency. Urgency is a tool designed to block thought. It overwhelms the mind. It pushes the living into decisions based on fear. Calm authority slows the pace. It refuses to act quickly. It demands proof. Proof takes time. Urgency collapses under time. The living protects themselves by refusing to rush.

Calm authority rejects intimidation. Intimidation is used when claimants lack evidence. They hope the living will submit to tone. They hope the living will fear the consequences. But intimidation is only effective when the living reacts emotionally. Calm authority removes emotion. It sees intimidation as a sign of weakness. It remains unmoved. This lack of reaction breaks the claimant's influence.

Calm authority focuses on truth. Truth is simple. Truth is steady. Truth does not depend on tone. Truth does not depend on pressure. Truth does not depend on fear. Truth stands alone. Calm authority aligns itself with truth. False authority cannot survive in the presence of truth. It is built on suggestion. Suggestion dissolves when truth appears.

Calm authority comes from understanding that the living is not required to engage in conflict. Conflict benefits false authority. It creates confusion. It creates noise. It creates distraction. When the living remains calm, conflict does not arise. Interactions stay focused on the claim. Claims must be proven. Without proof, they fall. Calm authority keeps the interaction on this simple, grounded path.

Calm authority is rooted in the recognition that the living has nothing to defend. People often feel they must defend their choices. They feel they must defend their presence. They feel they must defend themselves against claims that have no evidence. Calm authority knows that nothing needs defending when truth is absent. If the claim cannot be proven, the living owes no defence.

Calm authority protects the living by refusing to add energy to false claims. False authority gains strength through reaction. It loses strength through calmness. When the living reacts emotionally, false authority grows. When the living remains calm, it weakens. This is the natural balance. Awareness creates calmness. Calmness dissolves illusion.

Calm authority recognises that the claimant often expects submission. They expect people to comply without question. They expect authority to be assumed. When the living displays calm authority, the claimant becomes unsure. Their expectations collapse. They must operate in truth or fail. Most fail.

Calm authority understands that authority must be shared between equals. False authority tries to position itself above the living. Calm authority does not accept this. It does not become aggressive. It does not try to dominate. It simply refuses to be below. This refusal is quiet. It is simple. It is steady. It places both individuals on equal ground. Equal ground weakens false authority.

Calm authority is also a form of self-respect. The living respects themselves enough to require truth. They respect themselves enough to stay grounded. They respect themselves enough to avoid emotional reactions. They respect themselves enough to refuse fear. Self-respect strengthens sovereignty. A sovereign being does not act from panic. They act from clarity.

Calm authority restores presence. Presence means the living is aware of every part of the interaction. They are not lost in fear. They are not lost in assumptions. They are not lost in confusion. They are here, steady, conscious. Presence makes manipulation impossible. Manipulation relies on the living being mentally absent. Presence closes that door.

Calm authority is not cold. It is not harsh. It is not uncaring. It is grounded. It is clear. It is pure. It comes from truth. Truth has no aggression in it. Aggression comes from fear. Calm authority has removed fear. What remains is certainty.

Calm authority becomes a habit. The more the living stands in truth, the easier it becomes. The artificial world loses its ability to provoke. The claimant's tools lose impact. The living becomes less reactive. They become more observant. They think clearly. They act only when truth supports action.

Calm authority ultimately protects the living because it prevents the artificial world from controlling the emotional state of the individual. Control begins with emotion. When emotion is controlled, behaviour follows. When behaviour follows, systems gain influence. Calm authority breaks this chain. It prevents emotional control. Without emotional control, no manipulation can take root.

Calm authority is not a technique. It is a state of being. It comes from understanding that nothing can bind the living without proof. Nothing can threaten the living without evidence. Nothing can force the living without consent. Once this understanding becomes natural, calmness becomes natural. And with calmness comes authority.

Calm authority stands because truth stands.

Truth does not fear questions.

Truth does not fear scrutiny.

Truth does not fear time.

When the living stands in calm authority, they cannot be moved by false claims.

They cannot be pressured.

They cannot be manipulated.

They cannot be controlled.

They stand.

They stay steady.

They stay sovereign.

Living Without Assumption

To live without assumption is to live with clarity. It is to walk through the world without allowing unproven claims to shape your actions. It is to remain aware of your own authority at all times. It is to meet every interaction with presence rather than habit. Most people live through assumption. They accept ideas without evidence. They obey instructions without questioning their origin. They believe statements that have never been proven. Assumption becomes their default. They live reactively. They live under invisible pressure. They live in a state of quiet fear. This is not natural. It is learned.

Living without assumption begins with questioning everything that seeks to influence your behaviour. Not with aggression. Not with suspicion. With clarity. Clarity asks the simple question, what is the proof. This one question dissolves the fog that assumption creates. Assumption needs darkness. Proof brings light. Once light enters, the shape of every interaction becomes visible.

Most people do not realise how much of their life operates under assumption. They assume certain roles outrank them. They assume written words must be obeyed. They assume official language carries authority. They assume silence creates obligation. They assume deadlines are mandatory. They assume threats are valid. They assume the recorded identity is the living being. Each assumption binds them. These bindings are invisible. They feel natural because they have existed since childhood. Living without assumption requires unlearning these behaviours. Unlearning begins with awareness.

Awareness means you see the difference between a claim and truth. A claim is a statement. Truth is what can be proven. Claims appear constantly. Truth appears only when asked for. The living who asks for truth does not allow claims to shape their behaviour. They act only when evidence stands behind the words.

Living without assumption removes pressure. Pressure is created by incomplete information. When a claimant makes a bold statement, the mind fills the gaps with fear. Fear creates urgency. Urgency leads to action before clarity. But pressure collapses when the living asks for proof. Proof removes the imagined consequences. When the living sees what is real, fear has no place to stand. This is why false authority fears questions. Questions break pressure.

Living without assumption also removes the tendency to react. Reactions come from habit. Habits trained by years of conditioning. A letter arrives. People react. A demand appears. People react. A threat is made. People react. Reaction is the opposite of sovereignty. Reaction comes from fear. Action comes from awareness. When the living stops reacting, they begin choosing. Choice restores authority.

Choice is central to living without assumption. Assumption removes choice. It creates automatic behaviour. Automatic behaviour allows systems to act without resistance. But when every interaction is met with awareness, choice replaces automation. The living decides whether to engage. They decide whether to respond. They decide whether to accept the terms. They decide whether the claim contains truth. This reintroduces freedom into every moment.

Living without assumption requires the living to stay present. Presence means you are here now, fully aware of yourself and the interaction. Most pressure operates on people who are not present. Their minds race. They imagine consequences. They rehearse possibilities. None of these are real. They are projections of fear. Presence dissolves projections. Presence reveals only what exists in the moment. Nothing more. Nothing less. Presence is clarity.

Living without assumption also requires patience. False authority tries to control pace. It wants quick compliance. It wants immediate agreement. It wants the living to act before they think. This is why many notices use urgent language. Urgency bypasses patience. Patience bypasses urgency. When the living takes their time, urgency loses power. Patience reveals truth. False authority cannot operate on someone who refuses to move until clarity appears.

Patience also protects the living from emotionally charged mistakes. Many interactions that seem threatening become harmless when given time. The living reads slowly. They observe. They ask for clarity. They do not rush. When truth appears, the decision becomes easy. Fear disappears. Action becomes simple. Living without assumption is not stressful. It is steady. It is controlled. It is clear.

Living without assumption means understanding the nature of proof. Proof is not something complex. It is not hidden. It is not difficult to request. Proof is simply evidence that supports a claim. Evidence removes uncertainty. Uncertainty creates fear. Fear creates compliance. The sovereign mind removes fear by removing uncertainty. Proof is the key.

Living without assumption requires the living to recognise the difference between direct experience and belief. Belief is inherited. Belief is taught. Belief is absorbed. Belief exists without evidence. Direct experience comes from observation. Observation is personal. Observation is real. When the living observes without assumptions, they begin to see that many claims contradict reality. The contradiction weakens false authority.

Consider the simple idea that the recorded identity binds the living being. People believe this without question. But direct experience reveals that the recorded identity is a representation created by others. It exists on paper. It exists in systems. It does not breathe. It does not think. Yet people treat it as themselves. This belief creates vulnerability. Living without assumption means separating the self from the record. The record can be used when beneficial, but it does not own the living.

Living without assumption means understanding that nothing becomes true simply because it is repeated. Repetition is one of the strongest forms of conditioning. Systems repeat the same phrases, the same warnings, the same statements. Over time, people accept repetition as proof. Repetition is not proof. Proof must come from evidence. Living without assumption breaks the spell of repetition. The living hears repeated words and asks for evidence. Repetition loses power.

Living without assumption requires recognising the difference between confidence and authority. Many claimants speak confidently. Confidence is not authority. Confidence is tone. Tone can be used to manipulate. Authority must be proven. When the living hears confidence, they look for evidence. If evidence is missing, confidence becomes irrelevant. Living without assumption removes the influence of tone.

Living without assumption also removes the fear of consequences. Many people obey because they fear the consequences of non-compliance. These consequences are rarely explained. They are implied. They are hinted at. They rely on imagination. Imagination creates fear. Fear creates action. But when the living asks for proof of consequences, the illusion breaks. False authority rarely describes consequences clearly because it cannot prove them. Living without assumption reveals this.

Living without assumption restores the living's ability to evaluate each claim independently. They no longer treat every notice as if it carries equal weight. They no longer assume that every statement has authority. They examine. They question. They observe. They require proof. This approach removes confusion. It removes panic. It removes overwhelm. Each claim becomes simple. It must stand or fall based on evidence alone.

Living without assumption requires the living to trust their own perception. Many people doubt themselves. They believe authority knows more. They believe others must be right. They believe questioning is dangerous. These beliefs come from conditioning. Conditioning teaches people to distrust their own understanding. The sovereign mind reverses this. It trusts its own clarity. It trusts its own awareness. It trusts its own observations. When the living trusts themselves, false authority loses control.

Living without assumption means refusing to accept internal pressure. People often pressure themselves based on imagined obligations. They believe they must meet expectations. They believe they must respond quickly. These internal pressures are inherited. They are not real. Proof removes these internal pressures. If the claim cannot be proven, the pressure collapses.

Living without assumption requires steady boundaries. Boundaries protect the living from external influence. Boundaries define what the living accepts and rejects. Boundaries define what the living engages with. Boundaries define the terms of every interaction. Assumption weakens boundaries. Proof strengthens them. A strong boundary is simple. It says, show the evidence or the claim does not apply.

Living without assumption turns the artificial world into a series of offers. Offers can be accepted or declined. Offers require agreement. Agreement requires consent. Consent requires clarity. Clarity requires proof. When the living sees claims as offers, the fear disappears. Fear is reserved for obligations. Offers do not create obligation. They create choice. Choice restores calm.

Living without assumption also reveals the simplicity of sovereignty. Sovereignty is not complex. It is not hidden. It is not dramatic. It is grounded presence. It is clarity. It is awareness. It is the refusal to act without understanding. It is the expectation that every claim must be proven. When the living embraces this, sovereignty becomes natural.

The artificial world becomes powerless when assumptions are removed.

False authority becomes visible.

Claims become simple.

Pressure becomes meaningless.

Fear dissolves.

What remains is truth.

What remains is clarity.

What remains is sovereignty.

To live without assumption is to return to your nature.

Your nature is calm authority.

Your nature is awareness.

Your nature is freedom.

Living without assumption is the way the living returns to themselves. It is the way the living steps out of fear. It is the way the living stops surrendering their authority to pressure, formality, or conditioning. To live without assumption is to live consciously. Conscious living dismantles false authority because false authority depends on unconscious behaviour. It depends on habits formed over years. It depends on the living acting automatically. Automatic action is the fuel of systems. Awareness removes the fuel.

Living without assumption begins with the recognition that nothing is true unless proven. People often mistake familiarity for truth. They see a familiar process and assume it must be legitimate. They see a familiar tone and assume it must be authoritative. They see familiar formatting and assume it must reflect lawful power. This belief is learned. It is not inherent. When the living questions these assumptions, the familiarity dissolves. What remains is the actual claim, stripped of illusion.

Living without assumption involves questioning the meaning of every statement that tries to shape your behaviour. Not because everything must be rejected, but because everything must be understood. Understanding prevents manipulation. Manipulation thrives when people accept statements without thinking. When the living requires clarity, manipulation ends. Clarity reveals whether the claim has substance. Many do not.

Living without assumption means examining how information is presented. The artificial world uses presentation to influence. It uses official formatting to create pressure. It uses bold text to create urgency. It uses structured layouts to create an illusion of order. These elements create emotional impact. They do not create truth. Presentation becomes irrelevant when proof is required. A well-designed document without evidence is nothing more than decoration.

Living without assumption requires attention to language. Language is used to create compliance. Words such as must, required, mandatory, outstanding, or owed are intended to provoke reaction. These words create expectation. They create pressure. But they do not create authority. Authority must be proven. Words alone cannot bind the living. When the living sees these words as emotional tools rather than truth, the pressure dissolves.

Living without assumption also requires awareness of tone. Tone can be used to intimidate. Claimants often adopt a firm voice to create the impression of control. They speak with certainty. They use unwavering language. But tone is performance. Performance collapses when questioned. Tone cannot replace truth. When the living sees past tone, the only thing left is the claim. The claim must be supported by evidence. Without evidence, tone is meaningless.

Living without assumption allows the living to step out of the recorded identity. The recorded identity is used as a net. It captures the living through habit. It draws them into roles created by institutions. When the living separates from the recorded identity, they see that many claims are directed at a label, not at them. Labels cannot respond. Labels cannot consent. Labels cannot be bound. When the living asks for proof that the claim applies to them, the connection must be shown. It rarely is.

Living without assumption challenges the foundation of implied obligations. Implied obligations arise from silence, speed, and habit. If the living responds quickly, systems treat the response as agreement. If the living remains silent, systems treat silence as consent. If the living acts without proof, the action becomes evidence of acceptance. These implied obligations dissolve when the living requires clarity before acting. Clarity must come first. Action follows only if truth supports it.

Living without assumption requires the living to slow down. Speed is a tool used by systems. They want decisions made quickly. They want compliance before reflection. They want responses before questions. When the living slows the pace, urgency collapses. Urgency cannot operate outside of confusion. Proof needs time. The living gives it that time. When time is given, truth rises to the surface and pressure falls away.

Living without assumption removes emotional entanglement. Many claims rely on emotional triggers. They aim to create guilt. They aim to create shame. They aim to create anxiety. These emotions cloud awareness. When awareness is clouded, the living becomes easier to influence. Living without assumption dissolves emotional triggers because the living is not responding to emotions. They are responding to truth. Truth is neutral. Truth is steady. Truth removes emotional manipulation.

Living without assumption means challenging internal voices that echo conditioning. Conditioning teaches people to obey without understanding. It teaches them to fear consequences that have not been shown. It teaches them to feel small when addressed by institutions. These internal voices are not the living. They are echoes of the system. When the living listens to themselves rather than the conditioning, the echoes fade. What remains is calm awareness.

Living without assumption restores personal authority. Personal authority is not force. It is clarity. Clarity gives the living the ability to choose without fear. Most people lose this ability because they believe they must act according to external expectations. Living without assumption removes these expectations. The living becomes centred. Centred individuals do not react to pressure. They act from truth.

Living without assumption reveals that most interactions with the artificial world are offers, not orders. Offers cannot compel. They require acceptance. Acceptance requires consent. Consent requires understanding. Understanding requires proof. This chain protects the living. When the living recognises that they have always been dealing with offers, the fear disappears. Offers can be declined. Declining is not rebellion. It is choice.

Living without assumption redefines how the living interprets consequences. Consequences appear large when unexamined. They appear inevitable when assumed. But when the living asks for proof of the consequences, most claims weaken. Many consequences exist only in the imagination. The artificial world thrives on imagined consequences. The sovereign mind thrives on truth. Truth exposes when consequences are real and when they are not. Real consequences can be addressed with clarity. Imagined consequences dissolve when faced with evidence.

Living without assumption creates internal peace. Peace does not come from avoiding pressure. It comes from understanding it. It comes from knowing that pressure often carries no truth. It comes from seeing that most claims depend on fear rather than on evidence. This understanding brings calmness. Calmness is strength. Calmness is clarity. Calmness protects the living more effectively than conflict ever could.

Living without assumption transforms the relationship between the living and the artificial world. The artificial world expects compliance. It expects assumption. It expects automatic behaviour. When the living no longer behaves automatically, the system loses control. It must now operate on truth or not at all. This forces claimants to be honest. It forces them to show their limits. It forces them to stand behind their words. Many cannot. When they cannot, their authority collapses.

Living without assumption simplifies life. Complexity thrives on assumption. Without assumption, complexity dissolves. Claims become simple. Interactions become clear. There is no need for elaborate arguments. There is no need to cite lengthy rules. There is no need to memorise processes. All that is needed is a simple question: what is the proof. This question is the filter that removes confusion. Everything must pass through it. Most things do not.

Living without assumption also strengthens boundaries. Boundaries define what the living accepts and what they reject. Boundaries prevent unwanted influence. Assumptions weaken boundaries by creating doubt. When doubt disappears, boundaries strengthen. A strong boundary is calm. It says, I require proof. If proof is not present, nothing passes the boundary.

Living without assumption removes noise. Noise comes from false claims. Noise comes from pressure. Noise comes from repeated statements that lack truth. When the living demands proof, noise becomes silence. It falls away because it cannot support itself. Only truth remains. Truth is quiet. Truth is steady. Truth does not demand attention. It simply exists. The living moves toward it naturally.

Living without assumption reshapes identity. When the living understands they are not the recorded identity, they become immune to emotional manipulation tied to names, numbers, and labels. They see the distinction. They see that the recorded identity belongs to the system. The living belongs to themselves. This separation protects them. It creates strength where there was once vulnerability.

Living without assumption means recognising that authority cannot be taken. It must be given. People give authority away when they act based on assumptions. When they stop assuming, authority returns to them. False authority shrinks. True authority reveals itself. True authority is always aligned with truth. Truth requires no deception. It needs no pressure. It needs no illusion. It stands alone.

To live without assumption is to live in truth.

Truth removes fear.

Truth removes confusion.

Truth removes pressure.

The living who stands in truth cannot be controlled.

They cannot be misled.

They cannot be intimidated.

They cannot be deceived.

They stand calm.

They stand aware.

They stand sovereign.

The Strength of Saying "Show Me"

There is a quiet strength in the simple phrase, show me. It is not confrontational. It is not aggressive. It does not create conflict. It does not resist for the sake of resisting. It asks for truth. Truth must be shown. If it cannot be shown, it does not exist. This is the essence of sovereignty. Sovereignty is not about fighting. It is not about opposing systems. It is not about winning arguments. It is about standing in truth, and truth is always revealed by proof.

The living who understands the strength of show me steps out of fear. Fear survives in silence. It grows when questions are not asked. It feeds on imagination. It thrives on assumption. Show me breaks the silence. It removes imagination. It replaces assumption with clarity. When the living asks for proof, they step into their authority. They stop reacting. They start observing. They stop complying automatically. They start choosing consciously.

Show me is powerful because it shifts responsibility. False authority always tries to place responsibility on the living. It tries to make the living justify themselves. It tries to make the living defend their actions. It tries to make the living explain why they should not comply. This reversal is deliberate. It keeps the living on the back foot. It keeps them uncertain. It keeps them vulnerable. When the living says show me, the reversal collapses. Responsibility returns to the claimant. The claimant must justify the claim. They must defend their position. They must show the evidence. Many cannot.

Show me exposes weakness with elegance. It does not attack. It does not accuse. It simply asks for truth. When truth is absent, the claimant's behaviour reveals it. They may avoid the question. They may change the subject. They may escalate the tone. They may use pressure. They may repeat themselves. They may become emotional. Each of these reactions is a sign that they do not have what you calmly asked for. Show me reveals this gently but firmly. It makes the invisible visible.

The artificial world depends on the living accepting claims without question. It depends on people believing that everything presented to them carries authority. It depends on the living entering agreements without knowing they are agreements. It depends on silence. Show me breaks this dependency. It brings everything into the open. When false authority is forced into the open, it cannot survive.

Show me keeps the interaction simple. Simplicity protects the living. Complexity is used to confuse. Confusion creates fear. Fear creates compliance. Show me cuts through complexity. It demands clarity. It asks for the origin of the claim. It asks for the basis of authority. It asks for the proof of obligation. If the claimant cannot provide these things, the living does not proceed. Simplicity dissolves confusion before it begins.

Show me also protects the living from emotional manipulation. Many claimants rely on tone, urgency, guilt, or intimidation. These tactics work only when the living reacts emotionally. When the living uses show me, they remain calm. Calmness defeats emotional pressure. Calmness brings truth forward. Truth does not need emotional force. It stands on evidence. Emotional pressure collapses under the weight of a single clear question.

Show me empowers the living by creating a boundary. Boundaries define the limits of what the living accepts. Without boundaries, false authority enters easily. When the living asks for proof, the boundary appears. The claimant must cross it. They must cross it with evidence. If they cannot, they cannot proceed. The boundary stands. The living remains protected.

Show me removes the idea that the living must explain themselves. They do not. Explanation is required only when truth has been shown. When the claimant provides clear evidence, the living can address it. When evidence is absent, the living has nothing to explain. They simply wait. Waiting reveals the truth as clearly as questioning does. If the claimant cannot show the basis for their claim, the claim dissolves naturally.

Show me reveals whether the claimant is acting from truth or from assumption. A claimant acting from truth welcomes the opportunity to provide evidence. They answer calmly. They offer clarity. They understand their own authority. A claimant acting from assumption avoids the question. They rely on tone. They rely on formatting. They rely on escalation. These differences become obvious when the living asks show me. Truth stands still. False authority tries to move quickly.

Show me restores equal ground. Many claimants expect to stand above the living. They expect obedience. They expect compliance. They expect their authority to be assumed. When the living asks for proof, the hierarchy collapses. The conversation becomes balanced. The claimant must behave as an equal, not as a superior. Equality weakens false authority. False authority needs imbalance to survive.

Show me protects the living from the assumption that the recorded identity binds them. When a claim is directed at a name, the living asks how the claim reaches them. They ask for evidence of agreement. They ask for proof of obligation. If the claimant cannot show the connection, the claim cannot bind the living. Show me reveals the distinction between the living and the record. This distinction protects the living from unwanted involvement.

Show me prevents the formation of silent contracts. Silent contracts arise when the living acts without understanding. When the living responds automatically. When they comply before clarity. These silent contracts are the foundation of false authority. Show me requires clarity before action. Action without clarity cannot occur. Silent contracts cannot form. This protects the living.

Show me neutralises escalation. Many claimants increase the severity of their language when questioned. They hope escalation will push the living into compliance. But show me remains calm. It does not react to tone. It does not react to threats. It does not react to urgency. It repeats its request. The repetition is steady. It exposes the emptiness of escalation. When escalation meets calm awareness, it loses all power.

Show me makes the claimant face the truth of their own position. If their authority is real, they can show it. If it is not, they cannot. False authority hopes this moment never comes. It hopes the living will comply without asking. When the living asks, the truth appears. The truth protects the living.

Show me strengthens the living's internal state. Each time the living uses it, they grow more confident. They see how claims crumble when questioned. They see how false authority retreats. They see how fear dissolves when faced with truth. This creates a positive cycle. Confidence grows. Calmness grows. Awareness strengthens. Sovereignty becomes natural.

Show me is the simplest form of self-respect. It says, I will not act without understanding. It says, I will not obey without evidence. It says, I will not give authority away. It says, I stand in truth. This self-respect does not need to be spoken loudly. It is felt in the tone of calmness. It is heard in steady questioning. It is shown through patience. False authority cannot penetrate self-respect grounded in truth.

Show me prevents intimidation from becoming influence. Intimidation requires compliance. When the living does not comply, intimidation becomes useless. It becomes obvious performance. Performance has no substance. It does not survive scrutiny. It dissolves in the light of proof.

Show me exposes manipulation. Manipulation depends on speed, confusion, and emotional reaction. When the living asks for proof, they slow down the interaction. They remove confusion. They remove emotion. Manipulation cannot operate in this environment. It becomes visible. Once visible, it loses effect.

Show me builds inner stillness. Stillness is the core of calm authority. Stillness is the foundation of sovereignty. Stillness allows the living to see the truth behind the claim. Stillness protects the living from noise. Stillness keeps the mind clear. When the living asks for proof, they step into stillness naturally.

Show me simplifies life. The artificial world presents many claims. They differ in tone, style, and formatting. When the living uses show me, every claim becomes the same. It must be supported by evidence. If it is not, it does not matter. This simplicity removes stress. It removes overwhelm. It removes confusion.

Show me reminds the living of their own authority. Authority is not something systems grant. It is inherent. It cannot be removed. It cannot be overridden without consent. When the living requires proof, they reclaim their authority. They stop acting from fear. They act from presence.

Show me is a return to truth. Truth stands without pressure. Truth stands without fear. Truth stands without manipulation. Truth stands because it is truth. When the living says show me, they align themselves with truth. False authority cannot survive this alignment.

Show me is simple, steady, powerful.

It protects the living.

It reveals the claimant.

It exposes illusion.

It restores sovereignty.

The living who says show me stands unshaken.

They stand aware.

They stand free.

Show me is not a challenge. It is not a refusal. It is not defiance. It is an invitation for truth to appear. When truth appears, clarity follows. When clarity appears, fear dissolves. When fear dissolves, sovereignty returns. This is the strength of show me. It is simple, but it transforms the entire interaction. The artificial world depends on people not using it. It depends on people accepting claims, demands, and expectations without question. Show me ends that pattern instantly.

Show me protects the living because it changes the direction of responsibility. False authority tries to push responsibility onto the living. It expects the living to carry the burden of explanation. It expects them to justify themselves. It expects them to act based on fear. Show me reverses the flow. It places responsibility back onto the one making the claim. The claimant must now carry the weight of their own words. Many cannot carry it.

Show me exposes the difference between truth and performance. False authority performs. It displays confidence. It uses tone. It uses formatting. It uses institutional language. These performances create the appearance of authority, not actual authority. Show me removes the performance and looks beneath it. If there is truth beneath the performance, it becomes visible. If there is nothing beneath the performance, the performance collapses.

Show me reveals motive. A claimant acting honestly will welcome the question. They will answer calmly. They will provide clear information. They will not try to escalate. They will not avoid the request. They will not pressure the living. They stand because their authority stands. A claimant acting through assumption reacts differently. They become uncomfortable. They try to regain control. They use tone. They use urgency. They use broad statements. These behaviours reveal that the claim is not supported by truth.

Show me strengthens the living's boundary. A boundary is the line that says, I require truth before I act. False authority tries to bypass this line. It tries to force the living into action through speed, fear, or habit. Show me reinforces the boundary. It makes the boundary visible. It makes the boundary firm. A clear boundary protects the living from being pulled into unwanted agreements. Without a boundary, the living becomes vulnerable to manipulation. With a boundary, manipulation has no place to enter.

Show me brings balance into the interaction. Many claimants assume they stand above the living. They act as though the living must obey them. They speak as though authority is inherent. They rely on this belief. Show me reveals that authority is not inherent. Authority must be proven. When the living asks show me, the claimant must stand on equal ground. This equality weakens false authority because false authority needs the illusion of hierarchy to function.

Show me prevents escalation from having influence. Escalation is one of the artificial world's favourite tools. When a claim is questioned, the claimant often increases the severity of their language. They hope escalation will cause panic. Panic leads to compliance. But escalation is meaningless without proof. When the living asks for evidence, escalation has nothing to stand on. It becomes empty noise. Show me transforms escalation into exposure.

Show me restores calmness. Calmness is the foundation of sovereignty. Calmness prevents emotional reactions. Emotional reactions are the doorway through which manipulation enters. When the living remains calm, they are immune to tactics that rely on fear or confusion. Show me keeps the interaction steady. It keeps the living centred. Centred individuals cannot be pushed. They cannot be intimidated. They cannot be deceived.

Show me keeps the living focused on truth rather than on threats. Threats distract the mind. They provoke imagination. Imagination amplifies fear. Show me directs the attention back to evidence. Evidence is solid. Evidence is clear. Evidence is not emotional. When the living focuses on evidence, threats lose force. Threats become irrelevant if they cannot be proven. This shift in focus protects the living from being manipulated through fear.

Show me encourages patience. Patience is a powerful form of strength. False authority depends on speed. It wants the living to act immediately. It wants the living to respond without thinking. Patience breaks urgency. Show me forces the claimant to slow down. It forces the interaction into a steady pace. A steady pace exposes truth. Truth does not need speed. Only false authority does.

Show me prevents the living from falling into confusion. Confusion is one of the artificial world's oldest tools. Confusion exhausts people. It overwhelms them. It makes them feel small. When people are confused, they surrender. Show me cuts through confusion. It demands clarity. Clarity destroys confusion. Once clarity appears, the living can see the shape of the interaction. They understand their position. They understand the claimant's position. Confusion fades.

Show me stops the living from stepping automatically into the recorded identity. Many claims depend on the living identifying with the name on the document. When the living sees the name, they react. They assume the claim applies to them. Show me interrupts this assumption. It asks the claimant to show how the claim connects to the living. If they cannot show this, the claim loses relevance. The living stays separate from the record. This separation protects them.

Show me dismantles the cycle of automatic compliance. Automatic compliance is the result of conditioning. People learn from a young age to respond immediately to authority. They learn to obey without question. This conditioning becomes habit. Show me breaks the habit. It creates a pause. The pause creates awareness. Awareness creates choice. Choice ends automatic compliance.

Show me reveals whether consequences are real or imagined. Many claims assign consequences that sound severe. They do this to create fear. But consequences must be proven. They must be grounded in legitimate authority. They must be supported by evidence. When the living asks show me, the claimant must present this evidence. If they cannot, the consequences do not exist. They are illusions generated by language. Once the illusion breaks, fear disappears.

Show me also prevents the living from internalising pressure. Pressure grows when people believe they must act immediately. They believe they must respond. They believe they must obey. These beliefs come from assumption. Show me removes the assumption. It replaces pressure with curiosity. It replaces urgency with stillness. It replaces fear with awareness. Awareness protects the living.

Show me builds confidence slowly and consistently. Each time the living asks for proof, they see how often it is missing. They see how often claims collapse. They see how often pressure disguises weakness. Each collapse strengthens their understanding. Confidence grows with experience. Confidence is not loud. It is quiet. It is steady. It is grounded in truth. This form of confidence cannot be taken from the living because it is built on reality.

Show me prevents the living from being overwhelmed by complexity. False authority uses complicated language. It uses multi-layered statements. It uses references to processes that the living does not understand. Complexity is designed to hide weakness. Show me simplifies everything. It asks for the core evidence behind the claim. If the claimant cannot show the core, the complexity becomes irrelevant. Complexity without substance is noise.

Show me protects the living from entering agreements unconsciously. Agreements require intention. Intention requires understanding. Understanding requires clarity. Clarity requires evidence. If clarity is missing, no agreement can be formed. Show me ensures this. It forces clarity before any step is taken. This protects the living from being bound by assumptions or silence.

Show me rebalances every interaction. The artificial world tries to dominate through presentation, tone, and urgency. Show me removes all three. It strips the interaction down to its truth. The claimant must show the authority behind the claim. If they cannot, the claim falls. The living remains untouched. This balance is what systems fear. They fear simplicity. They fear awareness. They fear calmness. They fear truth.

Show me makes sovereignty practical. Sovereignty is not an idea. It is a behaviour. It is the way the living moves through the world. It is the way they speak. It is the way they think. Sovereignty is simple. It is the refusal to act without proof. It is the refusal to accept illusion. It is the refusal to surrender authority. Show me embodies this behaviour perfectly. It is the heart of practical sovereignty.

Show me reveals the truth behind every claim.

False authority cannot survive it.

Illusion cannot withstand it.

Fear cannot influence it.

Confusion cannot distract it.

116

The living who asks show me stands in truth.

They stand in clarity.

They stand in sovereignty.

They stand free.

The Quiet Power of Proof

Proof is quiet. It does not shout. It does not demand attention. It does not pressure anyone. It does not use intimidation. It does not rely on appearance. Proof stands calmly because truth stands calmly. False authority needs noise to survive. It needs urgency. It needs formality. It needs the appearance of certainty. Proof needs none of these. Proof speaks only when asked. And when it speaks, it ends illusion immediately.

The quiet power of proof protects the living more effectively than conflict ever could. Conflict drains energy. Conflict strengthens false authority because false authority knows how to respond to resistance. It is prepared for anger. It is prepared for confrontation. It is even prepared for refusal. It is not prepared for stillness. It is not prepared for calm questioning. It is not prepared for a simple request that exposes its weakness. The living does not need force. They need clarity. Proof provides clarity.

The quiet power of proof works because it brings everything into the open. False authority hides behind assumptions. It hides behind tone. It hides behind scripts. It hides behind complexity. When the living asks for proof, these hiding places disappear. A claim must stand on its own. If it cannot stand, it falls. The fall is gentle but irreversible. A weak claim cannot survive exposure to truth.

The quiet power of proof protects the living by ending uncertainty. Uncertainty is the root of fear. When a claim is vague, fear fills the empty space. When a message is unclear, imagination creates consequences. These consequences feel real. They shape behaviour. False authority depends on this. Proof ends uncertainty. It demands specifics. Specifics reveal whether the claim has substance. If it has no substance, uncertainty vanishes. Fear vanishes with it.

The quiet power of proof allows the living to remain calm. Calmness is essential. Most people face claims with anxiety. They feel pressured. They feel judged. They feel threatened. This pressure is the fuel that drives compliance. But when the living asks for proof, calmness replaces anxiety. There is no need to fear a claim that cannot be proven. Calmness comes from understanding this. Calmness gives the living the ability to think clearly. Thinking clearly dismantles illusion.

The quiet power of proof simplifies life. Many people become overwhelmed by the artificial world. They feel trapped in its demands. They feel they must keep up with every instruction, notice, or warning. They believe everything must be addressed urgently. This belief is incorrect. Most claims cannot survive a simple request for truth. Proof is the filter. Anything that passes through the filter deserves attention. Anything that does not pass through the filter does not matter. This simplicity removes stress.

The quiet power of proof reveals the difference between authority and appearance. Appearance can be created. Authority must be shown. Many claimants rely on appearance. They rely on uniformity. They rely on formatting. They rely on official words. These appearances give the impression of power. But appearance collapses when asked for the evidence behind it. When appearance collapses, the claimant must reveal what is real. If nothing is real, appearance becomes irrelevant.

The quiet power of proof protects the living from automatic compliance. Automatic compliance is the condition people fall into when they do not question. It is the condition created by years of conditioning. Automatic compliance is a habit. Proof interrupts the habit. It forces the living to pause. It forces them to reflect. The pause breaks the cycle. The moment the living asks for proof, they step out of automatic behaviour. That step is sovereignty.

The quiet power of proof protects the living from manipulation. Manipulation relies on emotion. Emotion bypasses thought. When people feel afraid, they do not question. When they feel ashamed, they do not think. When they feel guilty, they do not pause. Proof redirects attention away from emotion and toward evidence. Evidence is not emotional. It is clear. It is concrete. It is steady. When the living focuses on evidence, manipulation has no entry point.

The quiet power of proof removes assumed hierarchies. False authority depends on people believing they are beneath those who make claims. It depends on people believing they must obey. When the living asks for proof, the false hierarchy collapses. The claimant must come down from assumed superiority and stand on equal ground. Equal ground removes illusion. Equal ground opens the door for truth. Equal ground protects the living.

The quiet power of proof strengthens presence. Presence means being fully aware of the moment. It means not being carried away by fear. It means not projecting imagined outcomes. It means seeing what exists and nothing more. Presence is natural when the living asks for proof. The question brings the mind back to the present. It removes noise. It removes distraction. It creates stillness. Stillness is where sovereignty lives.

The quiet power of proof transforms the relationship between the living and the artificial world. The artificial world relies on the assumption that its claims will be accepted. It relies on unspoken agreements. It relies on obedience without thought. When the living demands proof, the system must operate differently. It must show evidence. It must reveal the truth. It cannot hide behind procedures. It cannot hide behind language. It cannot hide behind repetition. Proof eliminates these hiding places.

The quiet power of proof protects the living from internal doubt. Doubt is used by systems to weaken people. Doubt makes people hesitant. Doubt makes them easy to influence. Doubt makes them believe they do not have the right to ask questions. But the living always has the right to ask. They always have the right to see evidence. When the living uses proof, their doubt fades. They see how often claims collapse. They see how often authority is assumed rather than proven. They see their own strength clearly.

The quiet power of proof protects the living from overload. The artificial world sends endless messages. Endless forms. Endless instructions. People feel overwhelmed because they believe everything carries equal weight. Proof sorts everything into two categories: what is real and what is not. Only what is real requires attention. Overload comes from treating everything as real. Proof removes this burden.

The quiet power of proof strengthens intuition. Intuition is not guesswork. Intuition is the deep recognition of truth and falsehood. Many people lose connection with their intuition because they have been taught to override it. They have been taught to trust authority over their own awareness. Proof restores this connection. When the living sees claims collapse repeatedly, they learn to trust the feeling that something is off. Intuition becomes an ally, not a doubt.

The quiet power of proof protects the living from emotional exhaustion. Emotional exhaustion happens when people respond to claims with fear, confusion, or stress. They drain themselves by reacting. Proof removes the need for reaction. It creates clarity. Clarity conserves energy. The living uses only the energy required for truth, not for illusion. This creates balance.

The quiet power of proof prevents silent agreements. Silent agreements form when the living acts without awareness. They form when people respond automatically. They form when people accept claims without question. Proof prevents silent agreements because it demands clarity before action. Action without clarity cannot be mistaken for consent. Proof creates intentionality. Intentionality protects the living.

The quiet power of proof reveals the shape of false authority. It shows where the claim is weak. It shows where the claimant avoids the question. It shows where pressure replaces evidence. It shows where intimidation is used instead of truth. Once the shape is visible, the claim cannot influence the living. Influence requires invisibility. Proof removes invisibility.

The quiet power of proof gives the living the ability to move through life peacefully. Peace does not come from avoiding conflict. Peace comes from understanding. When the living understands how claims operate, they no longer fear them. They see through them. They address only what is real. They ignore what is not. This brings calmness. Calmness brings steadiness. Steadiness brings confidence.

The quiet power of proof is not about winning. It is not about defeating anyone. It is not about proving superiority. It is about making truth the standard. When truth is the standard, illusion has no place. When illusion has no place, sovereignty becomes natural.

The quiet power of proof returns the living to their nature.

Their nature is awareness.

Their nature is clarity.

Their nature is freedom.

Where proof stands, fear falls.

Where truth stands, illusion ends.

Where clarity stands, sovereignty begins.

The living stands in truth.

The living stands in clarity.

The living stands sovereign.

The quiet power of proof is the foundation of living consciously. It is the method by which the living steps out of illusion and into clarity. It is the anchor that prevents fear from controlling behaviour. It is the filter that separates truth from appearance. It is the light that exposes false authority. It is the tool that protects the living in every interaction. Once the living understands this, they will never return to assumption. They will never return to automatic compliance. They will never return to fear.

The quiet power of proof works because it is based on truth, not emotion. Truth does not require shouting. Truth does not require force. Truth does not need to dominate. It stands quietly. When the living aligns themselves with truth, they gain the same quiet strength. They become steady. They become calm. They become aware. They stop reacting to noise. They stop falling into traps set by fear. They stop being pulled into illusions created by systems.

The quiet power of proof creates a new way of seeing the world. Instead of seeing authority where there is none, the living sees only claims. Instead of seeing commands, they see requests. Instead of seeing threats, they see attempts to create compliance. Instead of seeing inevitability, they see choice. This shift is profound. It transforms how the living moves through life. It gives them internal stability. It gives them clarity that cannot be taken away.

The quiet power of proof reveals that many claims are built on expectation, not authority. The artificial world relies on people behaving in predictable ways. It relies on people responding automatically. It relies on people believing that everything placed in front of them must be obeyed. When the living asks for proof, they break this expectation. They refuse to follow the script written by others. This refusal is not defiance. It is awareness.

The quiet power of proof restores personal boundaries. Personal boundaries are essential to sovereignty. Without boundaries, the living becomes vulnerable to external influence. They become vulnerable to pressure. They become vulnerable to manipulation. Boundaries define what the living accepts. Proof becomes the gatekeeper. If a claim cannot present evidence, it cannot cross the boundary. This gatekeeping protects the living not through aggression, but through clarity.

The quiet power of proof brings integrity into interactions. Many claimants do not operate from truth. They operate from habit. They operate from script. They operate from assumption. When the living asks for evidence, the claimant is forced into honesty. They cannot rely on tone. They cannot rely on procedure. They cannot rely on confidence. They must show the truth or withdraw. This shift forces integrity.

The quiet power of proof protects the living from internalised authority. Internalised authority is when people believe they must obey because they have been taught to obey. They obey the tone. They obey the formatting. They obey the idea of authority, even when no authority exists. Living with the quiet power of proof removes this programming. It replaces obedience with clarity. It replaces fear with calmness. It replaces automatic reactions with intentional ones.

The quiet power of proof brings stillness into situations where people would normally panic. Panic is the tool of false authority. People panic when they believe they have no choice. They panic when they believe a claim is absolute. They panic when they believe the consequences are real. Proof dissolves panic. It asks, what is the truth. When the living sees the truth, panic fades. There is nothing to fear when the claimant cannot show evidence.

The quiet power of proof protects the living from overwhelm. Overwhelm occurs when people believe they must handle everything placed before them. They try to manage every notice, every demand, every instruction. This leads to stress. Stress leads to confusion. Confusion leads to compliance. But the quiet power of proof sorts everything. Only claims supported by evidence deserve attention. Everything else falls away. This creates simplicity. Simplicity brings peace.

The quiet power of proof strengthens the living's internal voice. Many people ignore their own instincts. They doubt themselves. They second guess their awareness. They believe others must be right. They believe systems must be correct. Proof restores trust in the self. When the living sees false claims fall apart, their confidence grows. They begin to trust their observations. They begin to trust their clarity. They begin to trust their own authority.

The quiet power of proof teaches patience. Patience is a rare strength in a world that rushes. But rushing benefits false authority. It prevents thought. It prevents clarity. It prevents truth from rising. When the living asks for proof, they slow everything down. They refuse to be rushed. They refuse to be intimidated by deadlines. They refuse to respond without understanding. Patience reveals truth. The claimant must either provide evidence or expose their own weakness.

The quiet power of proof transforms fear into observation. Fear narrows the mind. Observation opens it. Fear assumes. Observation sees. When the living observes rather than reacts, they can see what is real. They see the claimant's tone. They see their avoidance. They see their inconsistency. They see their reliance on appearance. These observations reveal the truth. Observation protects the living because it prevents emotional manipulation.

The quiet power of proof removes guilt. Many claimants use guilt as a tool. They suggest the living has done something wrong. They suggest the living is responsible. They suggest the living must explain themselves. Guilt creates vulnerability. Vulnerability creates compliance. Proof removes guilt by demanding evidence. If there is no evidence of wrongdoing, guilt is baseless. The living refuses to carry what is not proven.

The quiet power of proof removes shame. Shame is used when guilt is not enough. Shame weakens people. It makes them feel small. It makes them act from fear. Proof dissolves shame. It asks for factual truth. Shame has no factual truth. It is a tactic, not evidence. When the living asks for proof, shame loses its influence. The living remains steady.

The quiet power of proof removes urgency. Urgency is manufactured. It is designed to force action. It is designed to prevent thought. It is designed to push the living into agreement. Proof stops urgency. It slows the interaction. It demands evidence, not speed. Speed cannot replace truth. When urgency meets proof, urgency collapses.

The quiet power of proof prevents false authority from gaining ground through repetition. Repetition is used to create belief. The same words appear again and again. People assume repetition means correctness. It does not. Proof exposes repetition for what it is another tactic. When the living asks for evidence, repetition becomes meaningless. A false claim repeated a hundred times is still false.

The quiet power of proof strengthens dignity. Dignity is lost when people allow others to pressure them. It is lost when they act from fear. It is lost when they surrender authority without awareness. Proof restores dignity. It says, I will not be treated as less than equal. It says, I will not obey without truth. It says, I stand in my own authority. Dignity is quiet but unshakable.

The quiet power of proof is the heart of sovereignty. Sovereignty is not noise. It is not shouting. It is not conflict. It is the refusal to accept illusion. It is the refusal to obey without evidence. It is the refusal to live through assumption. It is the steady demand for truth.

The quiet power of proof allows the living to walk through the artificial world without fear.

They see claims for what they are.

They see the difference between truth and noise.

They remain calm.

They remain aware.

They remain in control of themselves.

The quiet power of proof ends manipulation.

It ends confusion.

It ends intimidation.

It ends unspoken contracts.

It replaces all of this with clarity, calmness, and sovereignty.

The living who walks with proof walks in truth.

They walk in awareness.

They walk in strength.

They walk sovereign.

Final Thoughts

Sovereignty is not a performance. It is not a fight. It is not a loud declaration. It is not a demand placed upon the world. Sovereignty is the quiet recognition of truth. Truth does not require force. It does not require threat. It does not require fear. Truth stands because it is truth. When the living stands in truth, they become unshakeable. They become grounded. They become aware. They no longer bend to pressure. They no longer fall into confusion. They no longer react from fear. They stand.

Proof is the foundation of this. Proof is the thread that runs through every interaction. It is the thread that brings clarity into situations designed to create confusion. It is the thread that reveals false authority. It is the thread that restores calmness. It is the thread that ends intimidation. It is the thread that protects the living from assumptions that would otherwise pull them into agreements they never made.

The modern world thrives on assumption. Systems rely on the belief that people will move quickly, obey without question, and accept claims without evidence. They rely on silence. They rely on habit. They rely on emotional reaction. When these foundations are removed, the entire structure shifts. A structure built on assumption cannot survive scrutiny. A structure built on pressure cannot withstand calmness. A structure built on fear cannot stand in the presence of truth.

The living who requires proof changes the interaction instantly. They stop the momentum of false authority. They interrupt the cycle of expectation. They bring everything back to clarity. This shift is powerful because it is simple. Simplicity is often overlooked. People expect power to be dramatic. They expect strength to be forceful. They expect sovereignty to be loud. But the strongest force in the world is clarity. Clarity destroys illusion without effort.

Requiring proof is not defiance. It is not rebellion. It is the natural state of the living. No one is born believing they must comply with statements made without evidence. That belief is learned. It is conditioned. It is taught through childhood, reinforced through schooling, and repeated through society. People learn to silence themselves. They learn to obey instinctively. They learn to accept appearance as truth. Requiring proof unlearns these behaviours. It returns the living to awareness.

Awareness is what separates the sovereign from those who live by assumption. Awareness means seeing the world as it is, not as fear imagines it to be. It means recognising when a claim is weak. It means understanding when someone is relying on tone instead of truth. It means feeling the difference between clarity and confusion. Awareness is natural, but conditioning dulls it. Proof restores it.

Proof also restores choice. Choice is the essence of freedom. True choice cannot exist in confusion. It cannot exist under pressure. It cannot exist in fear. When the living requires proof, they create space. In that space, they see clearly. They decide from clarity, not confusion. They decide from truth, not assumption. They decide from understanding, not fear. This space is where sovereignty lives.

People often believe they have no choice because they see claims as commands. They see letters as orders. They see statements as law. This belief is not based on truth. It is based on habit. When the living asks for proof, claims become offers. Offers can be accepted or declined. The living chooses. This simple shift in perception disarms false authority completely.

Requiring proof also dissolves the illusion of hierarchy. The artificial world depends on the belief that some people have inherent authority over others. This belief is not based on truth. Authority must be proven. It cannot be assumed. When the living asks for proof, the assumed hierarchy collapses. The claimant must stand on equal ground. Equal ground reveals truth. Truth reveals limits. Many people who act with confidence do so only because they expect no one to question them. When questioned, their confidence fades. Their authority shrinks. Their claims reveal their weakness.

Throughout life, the living will encounter many claims. Some will be polite. Some will be aggressive. Some will be vague. Some will be overwhelming. The common thread is expectation. Expectation that the living will obey. Expectation that they will react emotionally. Expectation that they will respond quickly. These expectations are the tools false authority uses to maintain control. Requiring proof breaks these tools. A claim cannot stand on expectation alone. It must stand on evidence. Evidence removes expectation.

Requiring proof does not create conflict. It creates clarity. Conflict arises when people do not understand their position. When they believe they must defend themselves. When they believe they must justify themselves. Requiring proof removes the need for defence. It removes the need for justification. It removes the need for conflict. The living does not argue. They ask for truth. The claimant either provides it or reveals its absence. Truth appears naturally. Conflict becomes unnecessary.

Requiring proof strengthens the living's internal world. Many people carry fear within them. Fear of doing something wrong. Fear of consequences that have not been shown. Fear of authority that has not been proven. Fear drains the living. It narrows their awareness. It makes them vulnerable. Proof dissolves fear by replacing imagination with reality. When the living sees that most threats are empty, fear fades. When fear fades, strength rises.

Requiring proof is not loud because truth is not loud. False authority is loud because it must be. Without noise, it would be exposed. Without urgency, it would be questioned. Without intimidation, it would lose control. Proof does not need to be loud. It asks simple questions. It waits. It observes. The living who uses proof becomes quieter over time. Their clarity grows. Their calmness deepens. Their presence strengthens.

Requiring proof reveals the nature of the recorded identity. The recorded identity is the point through which most claims attempt to reach the living. Many people believe the recorded identity is who they are. This belief creates vulnerability. When the living asks for proof of how the claim connects to them, the separation becomes visible. The separation protects them. The recorded identity belongs to the artificial world. The living belongs to the living. Proof is the key that maintains this distinction.

Requiring proof builds resilience. Resilience is the ability to remain steady in the presence of pressure. It is the ability to think clearly when confronted with uncertainty. It is the ability to stay calm when others try to influence your behaviour. Proof creates resilience because it brings reality into focus. When the living sees truth, they are not moved by pressure. They are anchored.

Requiring proof teaches the living to trust themselves. Self-trust is essential for sovereignty. Without self-trust, people fall easily into fear. They doubt their own understanding. They assume others know more. Proof restores self-trust by showing how often clarity comes from within. The living sees how their instincts align with truth. Confidence grows quietly. Self-trust becomes strong.

Requiring proof dismantles the belief that authority is external. True authority comes from within. It comes from knowing the difference between claim and truth. It comes from calmness. It comes from awareness. It comes from stillness. It does not come from titles, uniforms, or formatting. It does not come from threats. It does not come from repetition. When the living understands this, external authority loses its hold.

Requiring proof is a lifestyle, not a tactic. It is the way the sovereign moves through the world. It is the way they engage with every interaction. It becomes natural. It becomes instinctive. It becomes effortless. As it becomes natural, fear disappears. Confusion disappears. Intimidation disappears. Pressure disappears. The living becomes steady. They become clear. They become unshakable.

Requiring proof returns the living to themselves.

It returns them to clarity.

It returns them to calmness.

It returns them to truth.

Truth is the foundation of sovereignty.

Truth is the protection of the living.

Truth is the end of illusion.

Truth is the beginning of awareness.

The living who walks with truth cannot be deceived.

They cannot be pressured.

They cannot be manipulated.

They cannot be controlled.

They stand in the quiet power of proof.

They stand in their own authority.

They stand sovereign.

Don't miss out!

Visit the website below and you can sign up to receive emails whenever Roger Davies publishes a new book. There's no charge and no obligation.

https://books2read.com/r/B-A-HHGNE-GQEKI

BOOKS 2 READ

Connecting independent readers to independent writers.

Did you love *I Require Proof: A Sovereign Guide to Breaking Presumption and Exposing False Authority*? Then you should read *I Do Not Consent: A Sovereign Guide to Standing in Your Own Authority*[1] by Roger Davies!

[2]

You were born free. You were not born as a record, a number, a role, or a function. You were born as the living man or the living woman. The world teaches you to forget this. Governments, councils, banks, and officials behave as though your silence is agreement. They behave as though your signature is automatic. They behave as though your consent exists even when you never gave it. Many people feel this pressure but do not have the words to express it. They know something is wrong. They know the system uses assumption. They know authority is taken through habit, not agreement.

This book speaks to those people. It speaks to those who already know they are sovereign. It speaks to those who refuse to live under silent contracts. It speaks to those who feel the artificial world pressing against them and want to stand in their own authority without fear.

---

1. https://books2read.com/u/mVzdv6

2. https://books2read.com/u/mVzdv6

I Do Not Consent is a clear and strong guide for the living being who wants to understand how modern systems claim power and how to withdraw consent calmly. It shows how institutions rely on presumption, confusion, roles, and unexamined behaviour. It explains how most authority is offered, not imposed. It shows how consent is taken through silence and how silence can be replaced with calm truth.

You will learn the difference between the living being, the recorded identity, and the assumed identity. You will see how institutions use these layers to bind the living without open agreement. You will learn how to separate yourself from roles that were never chosen. You will learn how to remove presumption, how to refuse unwanted authority, how to stand as the living, and how to protect your own inner freedom.

This book does not teach conflict. It teaches clarity. It teaches calm presence. It teaches simple actions that prevent silent contracts. It teaches how to speak from the living and how to question claims that rely on pressure instead of proof. It shows how fear is used to control behaviour and how to replace that fear with steady awareness.

Every idea in this work is written for people who already feel the pull toward sovereignty. It strengthens that pull. It clarifies it. It supports it. It gives structure to what many already sense within themselves. It is for those who know they do not belong to any system. It is for those who choose their own path. It is for those who say the words I do not consent and mean them.

If you want to understand how the system operates without attacking it, this book shows you.If you want to stand as the living without confusion, this book guides you.If you want to speak truth without fear, this book strengthens you.If you want to reclaim your own authority, this book supports you.

You do not need permission to be sovereign.You do not need approval to stand as the living.You do not need fear to guide your choices.

Your authority begins with you.Your consent belongs to you.Your path belongs to you.

I Do Not Consent is written for those who already know this and want to live it with clarity and strength.

Also by Roger Davies

Adventures in Sovereignty: Growing Up Free
The Secret of the Hidden Name

Sovereign Action
Cease the Decree: Ending Contracts in Peace
I Do Not Consent: A Sovereign Guide to Standing in Your Own Authority
Council Tax Nullity: How to Challenge Local Tax Demands through Honour and Law
I Require Proof: A Sovereign Guide to Breaking Presumption and Exposing False Authority
The Private Record: How to Build Lawful Evidence of Truth and Standing
I Stand Recorded: A Sovereign Guide to Notice, Response and Written Authority

Sovereign Foundations: Liberty, Rights, Consent
The Constitution of One: How the Bill of Rights Protects the Sovereign Man & Woman
From Subjects to Sovereigns: Reclaiming the Spirit of 1776
Liberty by Consent: Reclaiming Freedom Through the Law of Consent

Standalone

The Commonwealth Corporation: How Australia Was Turned Into a Business
The Legal Fiction: The Greatest Trick Ever Played on Humanity
The Sovereign Path: Living Free Beyond the System
Common Law: The True Law of the Living
Freedom by Rebuttal: How to Say No and Stand Free
The Magna Carta: Why It Is Important to Sovereign Men and Women
The Trust Game: Hidden Estates and the Cestui Que Vie Act
Freedom by Notice: Winning with Paperwork
The Hidden Contracts: How Governments Enslave the People
The Law of the Living: Admiralty Shadows and the Path to Sovereignty
Standing as a Living Man or Woman in Canada: Reclaiming Freedom Beyond Statutes and Policy
Sovereign Stories for Children: 14 Parables of Freedom, Truth, and Honour
The Definitive Sovereign Handbook: Do No Harm, Cause No Loss, Commit No Fraud
Lose the Fear: Be Sovereign and Free
Sovereign 2026: Losing the Fear
When Council Tax Fear Takes Over: How to steady your mind and regain your internal peace
The Truth Movement: Breaking Presumption, Reclaiming Freedom, Living as Sovereign
Common Law Courts and Sheriffs: Restoring the Authority of the People

About the Author

Roger Davies researches the crossroads of commerce, policy, and personal sovereignty. He writes for readers who sense there is more to the story, who are ready to replace fear with honour and paperwork with plain truth. When not writing, he helps men and women organise their records, challenge unfounded claims, and build communities grounded in mutual aid and responsibility.

www.ingramcontent.com/pod-product-compliance
Lightning Source LLC
LaVergne TN
LVHW022055200926
848481LV00003B/928
9798232030704